W9-BKC-834

In this sixth book in the Spelling and Writing Together series, children continue to practice new spelling words as they strengthen their writing skills. They organize paragraphs that describe, provide examples, and tell what happened in the order it occurred. They separate fact from opinion, write from different points of view, and write persuasively. Other lessons help children learn to write poetry, instructions, and stories. The lessons stress the writing process: brainstorming ideas, putting them in order, writing a draft, making corrections, and writing a final version. Note: The letters that are written between two lines are sounds. For example, /k/ is the sound for the letters k and c.

Table of Contents

Glossary

Adjective. A word that discribes nouns.

Adverb. A word that tells something about a verb.

Analogy. Shows a relationship between two pairs of words.

Apostrophe. A punctuation mark that shows possession (Kim's hat) or takes the place of missing letters in a word (isn't).

Consonants. All the letters except **a, e, i, o, u,** and sometimes **y**.

Fact. A true statement. Something that can be proved.

Homophones. Words that sound alike but have different spellings and meanings.

Joining Words (Conjunctions). Words that join sentences or combine ideas: **and, but, or, because, when, after, so**.

Metaphor. A comparison of two unlike things without the words **like** or **as**.

Noun. A word that names a person, place, or thing.

Opinion. What someone thinks or believes.

Paragraph. A group of sentences that tells about one main idea.

Plural. A word that refers to more than one thing, such as a plural noun or verb.

Possessive Noun. A noun that owns something, such as **Jill's** book or the **women's** hair.

Prefix. One or two syllables added to the beginning of a word to change its meaning.

Pronoun. Words that can be used in place if a noun, such as **I, she, it,** and **them**.

Question. A sentence that asks something.

Simile. A comparison of two unlike things using the words **like** or **as**.

Singular. A word that refers to only one thing, such as a singular noun or verb.

Statement. A sentence that tells something.

Subject. A word or several words that tell whom or what a sentence is about.

Suffix. One or two syllables added to the end of a word.

Syllable. A word—or part of a word—with only one vowel sound.

Synonym. A word that means the same thing as another word.

Verb. The action word in a sentence; the word that tells what something does or that something exists.

Name: _____

Spelling Words With ie And ei

Many people have trouble deciding whether to spell a word **ie** or **ei**, with good reason. The following rules have many exceptions, but they may be helpful to you. If the two letters are pronounced /ē/ and are preceded by an /s/ sound, spell them **ei**, as in rec**ei**ve. If the two letters are pronounced /ē/ but are not preceded by an /s/ sound, spell them **ie** as in bel**ie**ve. If the letters are pronounced /ā/, spell them **eigh** as in **eight** or **ei** as in v**ei**n. If the letters are pronounced /ī/, spell them **eigh** then, too, as in h**eigh**t.

Directions: Use the words from the word box in these exercises.

veil	brief	deceive	belief	niece
vein	reindeer	yield	achieve	height
neighbor	seize	grief	ceiling	weight

1. Write each word in the row that names at least one of its vowel sounds.
    (One word will be listed twice.)

/sē/ _____

/ē/ _____

/ā/ _____

/ī/ _____

2. Finish each sentence with a word that has the vowel sound given. Use each word from the word box only once.

My next door /ā/ _____ wore a long /ā/ _____ at her wedding.

Will the roof hold the /ā/ _____ of Santa's /ā/ _____ ?

My nephew and /ē/ _____ work hard to /ē/ _____ their goals.

I have a strong /ē/ _____ they would never /ē/ _____ me.

For a /ē/ _____ moment, I thought Tim would /ē/ _____ the game to me.

The blood rushed through my /ā/ _____ .

What is the /ī/ _____ of this /ē/ _____ ?

The thief was going to /ē/ _____ the money!

Name: _____

Writing Four Kinds Of Sentences

Remember the four main kinds of sentences:

A **statement** tells something.

A **question** asks something.

A **command** tells someone to do something.

An **exclamation** shows strong feeling or excitement.

FOUR KINDS OF SENTENCES.

Directions: Write what you would say in each situation below. Then tell whether the sentence you wrote was a statement, question, command, or exclamation. Write at least one of each. Be sure to use periods after statements and commands, question marks after questions, and exclamation marks after exclamations.

Like this:

Write what you might say to a friend who's late to school:

Why are you late? .... question

Boy, are you in trouble! .... exclamation

Write what you might say to:

1. A friend who studied all night for the math test

_____ _____

2. Your teacher about yesterday's homework

_____ _____

3. A child you're watching who won't sit still for a brief second

_____ _____

4. Your sister, who's been on the phone too long

_____ _____

5. A strange kid who just seized your bike

_____ _____

6. A friend who's carrying a big box

_____ _____

7. Your dad, who's trying to lose weight

_____ _____

8. A friend who's been teasing you about your height

_____ _____

Name: _____

Figuring Out Homophones

Homophones are two words that sound the same, but have different spellings and different meanings. Here are several homophones: night/knight, fair/fare, not/knot.

Directions: Finish each sentence with the correct homophone.
Then write another sentence using the other homophone in the pair.

Like this:

Eight/ate   So far i <u>ate</u> two cookies.

Joanie had <u>eight</u> cookies!

1. Vein/vain

Since the newspaper printed his picture, Andy has been so self-centered and _____.

_____

2. Weight/wait

We had to _____ a long time for the show to start.

_____

3. Weigh/way

He always insists that we do it his _____.

_____

4. Seize/seas

The explorers charted the _____.

_____

Directions: Write each word from the word box next to the way it's pronounced.

veil	brief	deceive	belief	niece
vein	reindeer	yield	achieve	height
neighbor	seize	grief	ceiling	weight

/bēlēf/ _____   /sēz/ _____   /nābər/ _____

/vāl/ _____   /rāndēr/ _____   /hīt/ _____

/wāt/ _____   /yēld/ _____   /grēf/ _____

/sēling/ _____   /dēsēv/ _____   /brēf/ _____

/achēv/ _____   /nēs/ _____   /vān/ _____

Name: _____

Knowing How To Use Sentence Parts

The **subject** tells whom or what a sentence is about.
   Sentences can have more than one subject: Dogs and cats make good pets.

The **verb** tells what the subject does or that it simply "is."
   Verbs can be more than one word: plays, is walking, had been said.

An **adjective** is a word or group of words that describes the subject or another noun.
   For example: cheerful, with blue spots.

An **adverb** is a word or group of words that tells how, when, where, or how often.
   For example: quietly, today, in a tree.

Directions: Mark how each underlined word or group of words is used in these sentences. Write **S** above the subjects, **V** above the verbs, **ADJ** above the adjectives, and **ADV** above the adverbs.

Like this:

   ADJ S   ADJ   V   ADV
   A <u>huge</u> <u>dog</u> <u>with long teeth</u> <u>was barking</u> <u>fiercely</u>.

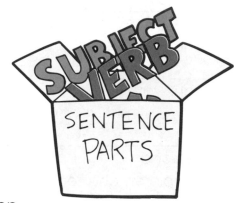

1. My <u>grandmother</u> <u>usually</u> <u>wore</u> a hat <u>with a veil</u>.

2. My <u>niece</u> and her <u>friend</u> <u>are</u> the <u>same</u> height.

3. The <u>lively</u> <u>reindeer</u> <u>danced</u> and <u>pranced</u> <u>briefly</u> <u>on the rooftop</u>.

Directions: Now write the sentences below, following the instructions. Mark each part you're asked to include. (If the parts of the verb get separated, mark each part.)

Like this:

   Write a question with two subjects, two verbs, and two adjectives:

  V   ADJ S   ADJ   S   V
   <u>Do the old dog and the frisky puppy play together?</u>

1. Write a statement with one subject, two verbs, and two adverbs:

_____

2. Write a command with one verb and two adverbs:

_____

3. Write a question with two subjects, two verbs, and an adjective:

_____

Name: _____

Using Math On Words

Directions: Add and subtract sounds to make new words. The new words may be spelled quite differently from the old words.

1. nice - /ī/ + /ē/ = _____

2. white - /ī/ + /ā/ = _____

3. size - /ī/ + /ē/ = _____

4. vine - /ī/ + /ā/ = _____

5. grief - /g/ + /b/ = _____

6. leaf - /l/ + /gr/ = _____

7. tail - /t/ + /v/ = _____

8. write - /wr/ + /h/ = _____

9. labor - /l/ + /n/ = _____

10. receive - /r/ + /d/ = _____

11. field - /f/ + /y/ = _____

12. sews - /ō/ + /ē/ = _____

13. wheat - /ē/ + /ā/ = _____

14. kite - /k/ + /h/ = _____

15. dealing - /d/ + /s/ = _____

16. shield - /sh/ + /y/ = _____

17. hate - /ā/ + /ī/ = _____

18. relief - /r/ + /b/ = _____

19. Kate - /k/ + /w/ = _____

20. breeze - /br/ + /s/ = _____

21. sale - /s/ + /v/ = _____

22. feeling - /f/ + /s/ = _____

23. beef - /b/ + /gr/ = _____

24. grease - /gr/ + /n/ = _____

25. heat - /ē/ + /ī/ = _____

Putting Ideas Together

We join two sentences with **and** when they are more or less equal:
   Julie is coming, **and** she is bringing cookies.

We join two sentences with **but** when the second sentence contradicts the first one:
   Julie is coming, **but** she will be late.

We join two sentences with **or** when they name a choice:
   Julie might bring cookies, **or** she might bring a cake.

We join two sentences with **because** when the second one names the reason for the first one:
   I'll bring cookies, too, **because** Julie might forget hers.

We join two sentences with **so** when the second one names a result of the first one:
   Julie is bringing cookies, **so** we won't starve.

Directions: Finish each sentence with an idea that fits with the first part.

Like this:
   We could watch TV, or _we could play Monopoly._____

1. I wanted to seize the opportunity, but _____

2. You had better not deceive me because _____

3. My neighbor was on vacation, so _____

4. Veins take blood back to your heart, and _____

5. You can't always yield to your impulses because _____

6. I know that is your belief, but _____

7. It could be reindeer on the roof, or _____

8. Brent was determined to achieve his goal, so _____

9. Brittany was proud of her height because _____

10. We painted the ceiling, and _____

Name: _____

Spelling Some Tough Words

Directions: Write in the missing letters in the words below.
If you have trouble, look In the word box on page 3.

Some people are dec_____ved into thinking that r_____ndeer aren't
real. Actually, r_____ndeer live in colder areas of North America and
other parts of the world. They reach a h_____ght of 2.3-4.6 feet at
the shoulder. Their w_____ght may be 600 pounds. When the
males battle, one of them y_____lds to the other.

My n_____ghbor had a stroke. One of his v_____ns burst in
his brain, so now he has trouble walking. Instead of being overcome
with gr_____f, he exercises every day so he can ach_____ve his goal of walking again.
I have a strong bel_____f that some day soon I will see him walking all by himself.

Directions: Only one word in each sentence below
is misspelled. Write it correctly on the line.

1. Fierce wolves hunt the raindeer. _____

2. My neice wore a long veil at her wedding. _____

3. My nieghbor is trying to lose weight. _____

4. Everyone gives me greit about my height. _____

5. His neighbor's house is beyond beleif. _____

6. The vain of gold yielded a pound of nuggets. _____

7. Trying to acheive too much can lead to grief. _____

8. She decieved us about how much weight she lost. _____

9. His niece is tall enough to reach the cieling. _____

10. A vale of water fell from a great height. _____

11. "That sign said, `Yeeld,'" the officer pointed out. _____

12. The worker siezed the box, despite its weight. _____

Name: _____

Review

Directions: Follow the instructions below to see how much you remember from the previous lessons. Can you finish this page correctly without looking back at the other lessons?

1. Write three words that spell /ā/ with ei. _____

2. Write a word that spells /ī/ with ei. _____

3. Write two words that spell /ē/ with ei. _____

4. Write a statement with one subject, two verbs, and an adverb. Mark them S, V, and ADV.

_____

5. Write a question with two subjects, one verb, and an adjective. Mark them S, V, and ADJ.

_____

6. Use the homophone for sealing in a command:

_____

7. Use the word pronounced /nēs/ in an exclamation:

_____

8. Finish these sentences in ways that make sense:

The ceiling fell down, but _____

The ceiling fell down because _____

The ceiling fell down, so _____

9. Find three misspelled words and write them correctly.

Todd breefly decieved me about what he was trying to acheive.

_____

Name: _____

Spelling Words With /ûr/ And /ôr/

The difference between /ûr/ and /ôr/ is clear in the difference between fur and for.

The /ûr/ sound can be spelled **ur** as in f**ur**, **our** as in j**our**nal, **er** as in h**er**, and **ear** as in s**ear**ch.

The /ôr/ sound can be spelled **or** as in f**or**, **our** as in f**our**, **oar** as in s**oar**, and **ore** as in m**ore**.

Directions: Use words from the word box in these exercises.

florist	courtesy	research	emergency	flourish
plural	observe	furnish	tornado	source
ignore	survey	normal	coarse	restore

1. Write each word in the row that names a sound in it.

/ûr/ _____

_____

/ôr/ _____

_____

2. Finish each sentence with a word that has the sound given. Use each word from the word box only once.

We all get along better when we remember to use /ûr/ _____ .

My brother likes flowers and wants to be a /ôr/ _____ .

What was the /ôr/ _____ of

the /ûr/ _____ for your report?

For a plural subject, use a /ûr/ _____ verb.

He waved at her, but she continued to /ôr/ _____ him.

Beneath the dark clouds was a /ôr/ _____ !

Firefighters are used to handling an /ûr/ _____ .

When will they be able to /ôr/ _____ our electricity?

How are you going to /ûr/ _____ your apartment?

Name: _____

Using Similes And Metaphors

A **simile** compares two unlike things using the words **like** or **as**. For example: The fog was like a blanket around us.

A **metaphor** compares two unlike things without the words **like** or **as**. For example: The fog was a blanket around us.

"The fog was thick" is not a simile or a metaphor. "Thick" is just an adjective. Similes and metaphors compare two unlike things.

Directions: In each sentence, underline the two unlike things being compared. Then mark the sentence **S** for simile or **M** for metaphor.

_____ 1. The florist's shop was a summer garden.

_____ 2. The wood was as coarse as sandpaper.

_____ 3. The survey was a fountain of information.

_____ 4. Her courtesy was as welcome as a cool breeze on a hot day.

_____ 5. The room was like a furnace.

Directions: Finish these sentences with similes.

1. The tornado was as dark as _____

2. His voice was like _____

3. The emergency was as unexpected as _____

4. The kittens were like _____

Directions: Finish these sentences with metaphors.

1. To me, research was _____

2. The flourishing plants were _____

3. My observation at the hospital was _____

4. Her ignoring me was _____

Name: _____

Searching For Synonyms

Directions: In each sentence, find a word or group of words that is a synonym for a word in the word box. Circle the word(s) and write the synonym on the line.

florist	courtesy	research	emergency	flourish
plural	observe	furnish	tornado	source
ignored	survey	normally	coarse	restore

1. The children seemed to thrive in their new school. _____

2. Her politeness made me feel welcome. _____

3. The flower shop was closed when we arrived. _____

4. The principal came to watch our class. _____

5. Are they going to fix up that old house? _____

6. Six weeks after the tornado, the neighborhood looked as it usually did. _____

7. What was the origin of that rumor? _____

8. The windstorm destroyed two houses. _____

9. She neglected her homework. _____

10. The material had a rough feeling to it. _____

11. Did you fill out your questionnaire yet? _____

Directions: Pick three of the words below and write a sentence for each one, showing you know what the word means. Then trade sentences with someone. Do you think your partner understands the words he or she used in sentences?

plural	flourish	source	restore	observe	furnish

1. _____

2. _____

3. _____

Name: _____

Creating Word Pictures

Directions: Rewrite each general sentence below two times, giving two different versions of what the sentence could mean. Be sure to use more specific nouns and verbs and add adjectives and adverbs. Similes and metaphors will also help create a picture with words. Notice how much more interesting and informative the two rewritten sentences are in this example:

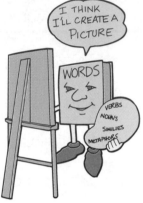

The animal ate its food.

<u>Like a hungry lion, the starving cocker spaniel wolfed down the entire bowl of food in seconds.</u>

<u>The raccoon delicately washed the berries in the stream before nibbling them slowly, one by one.</u>

1. The person built something.

_____

_____

2. The weather was bad.

_____

_____

3. The boy went down the street.

_____

_____

4. The helpers helped.

_____

_____

5. The bird flew to the tree.

_____

_____

Name: _____

Using Different Forms Of Verbs

To explain what is happening right now, we can use a "plain" verb or we can use **is** or **are** and add **-ing** to a verb.
Like this: We enjoy. They are enjoying.

To explain something that already happened, we can add **-ed** to many verbs or we can use **was** or **were** and add **-ing** to a verb.
Like this: He surveyed. The workers were surveying.

Remember to drop the final **e** on verbs before adding another ending and to add **-es** instead of just **-s** to verbs that end with **sh** or **ch**.
Like this: She is restoring. He furnishes.

Directions: Finish each sentence with the correct form of the verb given. Some sentences already have **is**, **are**, **was**, or **were**.

1. The florist is (have) a sale this week. _____

2. Last night's tornado (destroy) a barn. _____

3. We are (research) the history of our town. _____

4. My mistake was (use) a plural verb instead of a singular one. _____

5. She (act) quickly in yesterday's emergency. _____

6. Our group is (survey) the parents in our community. _____

7. For our last experiment, we (observe) a plant's growth for two weeks. _____

8. A local company already (furnish) all of the materials for this project. _____

9. Which dairy (furnish) milk to our cafeteria every day? _____

10. Just (ignore) the mess in here. _____

11. I get so angry when he (ignore) me. _____

12. Our town is (restore) some old buildings. _____

13. This fern grows and (flourish) in our bathroom. _____

14. Well, it was (flourish) until I overwatered it. _____

Name: _____

Describing People

Directions: Often we can show our readers how someone feels by describing how that person looks or what he or she is doing. Read the phrases below. Write in a word or two to show how you think that person feels.

1. Like a tornado, yelling, raised fists: _____

2. Slumped, walking slowing, head down: _____

3. Trembling, breathing quickly, like a cornered animal: _____

Directions: Write two or three sentences to describe how each person below feels. Don't name any emotions, such as angry, excited, or frightened. Instead, tell how the person looks and what he or she is doing. Create a picture with specific nouns and verbs, plus adjectives, adverbs, similes, and metaphors.

1. a runner who has just won a race for his or her school

_____

_____

2. someone on the first day in a new school

_____

_____

3. someone walking down the street and spotting a house on fire

_____

_____

4. a scientist who has just discovered a cure for lung cancer

_____

_____

5. a person being ignored by his or her best friend

_____

_____

Name: _____

Spelling Plurals

Is it hero**s** or hero**es**? Many people aren't sure. Although these rules have exceptions, they will help you spell the plural forms of words that end with **o**:

If a word ends with a consonant and **o**, add **-es**: hero**es**.
If a word ends with a vowel and **o**, just add **-s**: radio**s**.

Don't forget other rules for plurals:

If a word ends with **s**, **ss**, **z**, **x**, **ch**, or **sh**, add **-es**:
buses, classes, quizzes, taxes, peaches, wishes.
If a word ends with **f** or **fe**, drop the **f** or **fe** and add **-ves**:
leaf, leaves; wife, wives.
Some plurals don't end with **-s** or **-es**: geese, deer, children.
The **-es** rule also applies when a word ending with
s, **ss**, **z**, **x**, **ch**, or **sh** is used as a verb:
kisses, mixes, teaches, pushes.

Directions: Write in the plural forms of the words given.

1. Our area doesn't often have (tornado). _____

2. How many (radio) does this store sell every month? _____

3. (Radish) are the same color as apples. _____

4. Does this submarine carry (torpedo)? _____

5. Hawaii has a number of active (volcano). _____

6. Did you pack (knife) in the picnic basket? _____

7. We heard (echo) when we shouted in the canyon. _____

8. Where is the list of (address) ? _____

Directions: Write the correct verb forms in these sentences.

1. What will you do when that plant (reach) the ceiling? _____

2. Sometimes my dad (fix) us milkshakes. _____

3. Every night my sister (wish) on the first star she sees. _____

4. Who (furnish) the school with pencils and paper? _____

5. The author (research) every detail in her books. _____

Name: _____

Review

Directions: Follow the instructions to see how much you remember from the previous lessons. Can you finish this page correctly without looking back at the other lessons?

1. Write three words that have the /ûr/ sound.

_____

2. Now write three words that have the /ôr/ sound.

_____

3. Finish this sentence with a simile:

   My bedroom is as neat as _____

4. Finish this sentence with a metaphor:

   My first day at school this year was _____

5. Use a synonym for crisis in a sentence.

_____

6. Create a "word picture" based on this sentence:

   The little boy washed his hands.

_____

_____

7. Write two or three sentences describing what a person who is worried about taking a test might look like and do. Show how the person feels without using the word "worried."

_____

_____

_____

_____

8. Rewrite this sentence, using an **-ing** form for the verb and the plural form of tornado:

   The winds from the tornado destroyed the trailer park.

_____

Name: _____

Spelling Words With /kw/, /ks/, And /gz/

The consonant **q** is always followed by **u** in words and pronounced /**kw**/. The letter **x** can be pronounced /**ks**/ as in mi**x**, but when **x** is followed by a vowel, it is usually pronounced /**gz**/ as in e**x**ample.

Directions: Use words from the word box in these exercises.

expense	exist	aquarium	acquire	request
exact	expand	exit	quality	excellent
quiz	quantity	exhibit	expression	squirm

1. Write each word in the row that names one of its sounds. (Hint: the **h** in exhibit is silent.)

/kw/ _____

_____

/ks/ _____

/gz/ _____

2. Finish each sentence with a word that has the sound given. Use each word from the word box only once.

We went to the zoo to see the fish /gz/ _____ .

I didn't know its /gz/_____ location, so we followed the map.

The zoo plans to /kw/_____ some sharks for

its /kw/ _____ .

Taking care of sharks is a big /ks/_____ , but a number of people

have asked the zoo to /ks/_____ its display of fish.

These people want a better /kw/_____ of fish,

not a bigger /kw/_____ of them.

I think the zoo already has an /ks/_____ display.

Some of its rare fish no longer /gz/_____ in the ocean.

Name: _____

Writing Free Verse

Poems that don't rhyme and don't have a regular rhythm are called "free verse." They often use adjectives, adverbs, similes, and metaphors to create word pictures like this one:

My Old Cat

Curled on my bed at night,
Quietly happy to see me,
Soft, sleepy, relaxed,
A calm island in my life.

Directions: Write your own free verse poems on the topics given.

1. Write a two-line free verse poem about a feeling. Compare it to some kind of food. For example, anger could be a tangle of spaghetti. Give your poem a title.

_____

_____

2. Think of how someone you know is like a color, sunny like yellow, for example. Write a two-line free verse poem on this topic without naming the person. Don't forget a title.

_____

_____

3. Write a four-line free verse poem, like "My Old Cat" above, that creates a word picture of a day at school.

_____

_____

_____

4. Now write a four-line free verse poem about dreaming at night.

_____

_____

_____

5. Write one more four-line free verse poem, this time about your family.

_____

_____

_____

Name: _____

Analyzing Words And Their Parts

Remember that a syllable is a word or part of a word with only one vowel sound.

Directions: Use the words from the word box in these exercises.

expense	exist	aquarium	acquire	request
exact	expand	exit	quality	excellent
quiz	quantity	exhibit	expression	squirm

1. Fill in any missing syllables in these words. Then write the number of syllables in each word.

ex_____lent ( )   ac_____( )   _____quest ( )   _____squirm ( )

quali_____( )   ex_____it ( )   _____act ( )   _____ it ( )

_____pense ( )   _____quiz ( )   ex_____sion ( )   _____pand ( )

_____quar_____um ( )   _____ist ( )   quan_____ty ( )

2. Write the word that rhymes with each of these words and phrases.

fizz _____   worm _____   the sand _____

resist _____   my best _____   the fence _____

in fact _____   good fit _____   on fire _____

made for me _____   reflection _____

it's been sent _____   this is it _____

3. Write in the word that belongs to the same word family as the one underlined.

I know <u>exactly</u> what I want; I want those _____ shoes.   _____

Those shoes look <u>expensive</u>. Can we afford that _____ ?   _____

She wanted us to <u>express</u> ourselves, but she still didn't like my _____ .   _____

When we went to the <u>exhibition</u>, I liked the train _____ best.   _____

The museum has a new <u>acquisition</u>. I wonder what they _____ .   _____

Writing Limericks

Limericks are five-line poems that tend to be silly. Certain lines rhyme, and each line usually has either five or eight syllables, like this:

There once was a young man named Fred	(8 syllables)
Whose big muscles went to his head.	(8 syllables)
"I'll make the girls sigh	(5 syllables)
'Cause I'm quite a guy!"	(5 syllables)
But instead the girls all liked Ted!	(8 syllables)

As you can see, all three 8-syllable lines rhyme, and the two 5-syllable lines rhyme.

Directions: Complete the limericks below.

1. There was a young lady from Kent
   Whose drawings were just excellent.

   _____
   _____

   And to the big city she went.

2. I have a pet squirrel named Squirm

   _____

   He ran up a tree
   As far as could be

   _____

3. There once was a boy who yelled, "Fire!"

   _____

   He just did not see

   _____
   _____

4. One day, I saw my reflection

   _____
   _____
   _____
   _____

Name: _____

Figuring Out A Crossword Puzzle

Directions: Read each definition and write the word that is defined in the spaces that start with the same number. If you need help with spelling, look in the word box on page 19.

Across

2. To show
5. A test
6. A cost
10. To obtain
11. To go out
13. To ask
15. To live

Down

1. To get bigger
3. A home for fish
4. Just right
7. Really good
8. How good something is
9. On your face
12. An amount
14. To wiggle around

Name: _____

Writing Acrostics

An acrostic is a poem written so the first letter of each line spells a word. The poem tells something about the word that is spelled out.

Here's an example:

I n the grass or underground,
N ow and then they fly around.
S lugs and worms and butterflies,
E ach has its own shape and size.
C aterpillars, gnats, a bee,
T ake them all away from me!

Directions: Write your own acrostic poems for the two words below. Then write a third acrostic poem for a word you select. You can make your poems rhyme or not rhyme, like free verse.

S _____

H _____

O _____

E _____

S _____

P _____

H _____

O _____

N _____

E _____

Write an acrostic poem here for the word you selected:

____ _____

____ _____

____ _____

____ _____

Name: _____

Finding The Spelling Mistakes

Directions: Find the spelling mistakes in each paragraph and write the words correctly on the lines. If you need help, look in the word boxes on pages 3, 11, and 19.

Sabrina wanted to aquire a saltwater acquarium. She was worried about the expence, though, so first she did some reseach. She wanted to learn the exxact care saltwater fish need, not just to exsist, but to florish. One sorce said she needed to put water in the aquarium and wait six weeks before she added the fish. "Good greif!" Sabrina thought. She got a kitten from her nieghbor instead.

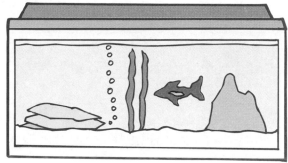

_____ _____ _____

_____ _____ _____

One stormy day, Mark was babysitting his neice. He happened to obsurve that the sky looked darker than norml. At first he ignorred it, but then he noticed a black cloud exxpand and grow in hieght. Then a tail dropped down from the twisting cloud and siezed a tree! "It's a toranado!" Mark shouted. "Maybe two toranados! This is an emergensy!" For a breef moment Mark wished he hadn't shouted because his niece looked at him with a very frightened expresion. Just then the cieling began to sag as if it had a heavy wieght on it. "This is an excelent time to visit the basement," he told the little girl as calmly as possible.

_____ _____ _____

_____ _____ _____

_____ _____ _____

Just before Mother's Day, Bethany went to a flourist shop to buy some flowers for her mother. "Well, what is your reqest?" the clerk asked. "I don't have much money," Bethany told him. "So make up your mind," he said impatiently. "Do you want quality or quanity?" Bethany wondered if he was giving her a quizz. She tried not to sqwirm as he stared down at her. Finally she said, "I want cortesy," and she headed for the exxit. The next time, she thought, I won't be decieved by a pretty exibit in the store window.

_____ _____ _____

_____ _____ _____

Review

Directions: Can you finish this page without looking back at the previous lessons?

1. Write three words that have the /kw/ sound.

_____ _____ _____

2. Write two words that have the /ks/ sound.

_____ _____

3. Write two words that have the /gz/ sound.

_____ _____

4. Write a limerick poem about yourself and your town.
   It might begin like this: "There was a boy from Columbus...." or
                                "There once was a girl from Belair...."

_____
_____
_____
_____
_____

5. Write an acrostic poem using the name of someone in your family and telling what you like
   about this person. Your poem can rhyme, but it doesn't have to. (Be sure to show it to that
   person.)

_____
_____
_____
_____
_____
_____
_____
_____
_____

Name: _____

Spelling Words With Silent Letters

Some letters in words are not pronounced. The ones you'll practice in this lesson include the **b** as in crum**b**, **l** as in ca**l**m, **n** as in autum**n**, **g** as in desi**g**n, and **h** as in **h**our.

Directions: Use the words from the word box in these exercises.

condemn	yolk	campaign	assign	salmon
hymn	limb	chalk	tomb	foreign
resign	column	spaghetti	rhythm	solemn

1. Write each word in the row with its silent letter.

/n/ _____

/l/ _____

/g/ _____

/b/ _____

/h/ _____

2. Finish these sentences with a word containing the silent letter given. Use each word from the word box only once.

What did the teacher /g/ _____ for homework?

She put words in a /n/ _____ on the board.

When she finished writing, her hands were white with /l/ _____ .

The church choir clapped in /h/ _____ with

the /n/ _____ .

While I was cracking an egg, the /l/ _____ slipped on the floor.

Did the explorers find anything in the ancient /b/ _____ ?

My favorite dinner of all is /h/ _____ .

Don't /n/ _____ me for making one little mistake.

Name: _____

Organizing Paragraphs

A topic sentence tells the main idea of a paragraph and is usually the first sentence. Support sentences follow it, providing details about the topic.

Directions: Arrange each group of sentences below into a paragraph that makes sense. Write the topic sentence first and underline it. One sentence in each group should not be included in the paragraph, so cross it out.

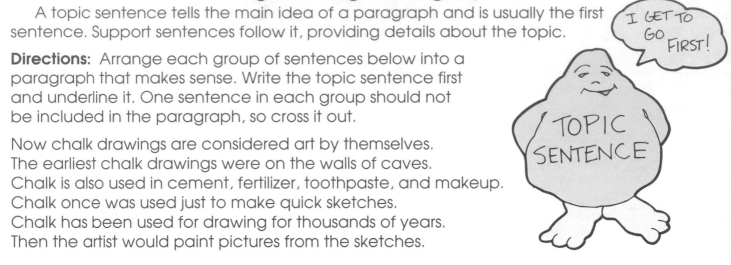

Now chalk drawings are considered art by themselves.
The earliest chalk drawings were on the walls of caves.
Chalk is also used in cement, fertilizer, toothpaste, and makeup.
Chalk once was used just to make quick sketches.
Chalk has been used for drawing for thousands of years.
Then the artist would paint pictures from the sketches.

_____

_____

_____

_____

_____

Dams also keep young salmon from swimming downriver to the ocean.
Most salmon live in the ocean but return to fresh water to lay their eggs and breed.
Dams prevent salmon from swimming upriver to their spawning grounds.
Pacific salmon die after they spawn the first time.
One kind of fish pass is a series of pools of water that lead the salmon over the dams.
Dams are threatening salmon by interfering with their spawning.
To help with this problem, some dams have special "fish passes" to allow salmon to swim over the dam.

_____

_____

_____

_____

_____

_____

_____

Name: _____

Analyzing Analogies

An analogy shows a relationship between two pairs of words.

An analogy might show that both pairs of words are synonyms:
talk is to **speak** as **expand** is to **grow**.

An analogy could also show that both pairs of words are opposites:
hot is to **cold** as **up** is to **down**.

A different analogy could show that one word is part of another:
paw is to **cat** as **fin** is to **fish**.

Directions: Write each word from the word box to finish these analogies. (Be sure to figure out the relationship between the first pair of words before finishing the analogy.)

condemn	yolk	campaign	assign	salmon
hymn	limb	chalk	tomb	foreign
resign	column	spaghetti	rhythm	solemn

1. **In** is to **out** as **joyful** is to _____ .

2. **Book** is to **novel** as **song** is to _____ .

3. **Cemetery** is to **casket** as **pyramid** is to _____ .

4. **Begin** is to **start** as **quit** is to _____ .

5. **Fast** is to **slow** as **native** is to _____ .

6. **Apple** is to **seed** as **egg** is to _____ .

7. **Dog** is to **collie** as **fish** is to _____ .

8. **Cheese** is to **pizza** as **sauce** is to _____ .

9. **Dish** is to **plate** as **beat** is to _____ .

10. **Knife** is to **scissors** as **crayon** is to _____ .

11. **Plant** is to **leaf** as **tree** is to _____ .

12. **Pick up** is to **collect** as **give out** is to _____ .

13. **Let go** is to **free** as **judge wrong** is to _____ .

Building Paragraphs

Directions:

1. Read each group of questions and the topic sentence.
2. On another sheet of paper, write support sentences that answer each question. Use your imagination!
3. Put your support sentences in order.
4. Read the whole paragraph out loud, make any necessary changes so the sentences fit together, and copy your sentences on this page after the topic sentence.

Questions: Why did Jimmy feel sad?
What happened to change how he felt?
How does he feel when he comes to school now?

Jimmy used to look so solemn when he came to school. _____

_____

_____

_____

_____

Questions: Why did Jennifer want to go to another country?
Why couldn't she go?
Does she have any plans to change that?

Jennifer always wanted to visit a foreign country. _____

_____

_____

_____

_____

Questions: What was Paul's "new way"?
Did anyone else like it?
Did Paul like it himself?

Paul thought of a new way to fix spaghetti. _____

_____

_____

_____

_____

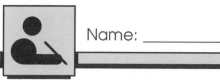

Name: _____

Matching Subjects And Verbs

If the subject of a sentence is singular, the verb must be singular.

If the subject is plural, the verb should be plural.

Like this: The **dog** with floppy ears **is eating**.

The **dogs** in the cage **are eating**.

Directions: Write in the singular or plural form of the subject in each sentence so that it matches the verb. If you need help spelling plural forms, look on page 17.

1. The (yolk) _____ in this egg is bright yellow.

2. The (child) _____ are putting numbers in columns.

3. Both (coach) _____ are resigning at the end of the year.

4. Those three (class) _____ were assigned to the gym.

5. The (lunch) _____ for the children are ready.

6. (Spaghetti) _____ with meatballs is delicious.

7. Where are the (box) _____ of chalk?

8. The (man) _____ in the truck were collecting broken tree limbs.

9. The (rhythm) _____ of that music is just right for dancing.

10. Sliced (tomato) _____ on lettuce are good with salmon.

11. The (announcer) _____ on TV was condemning the dictator.

12. Two (woman) _____ are campaigning for mayor of our town.

13. The (group) _____ of travelers was on its way to three foreign countries.

14. The (choir) _____ of thirty children is singing hymns.

15. In spite of the parade, the (hero) _____ were solemn.

Name: _____

Explaining With Examples

Some paragraphs describe people, places, or events using adjectives, adverbs, similies, and metaphors, like the paragraphs you wrote on page 16. Other paragraphs explain by naming examples, like this one:

Babysitting is not an easy way to earn money. For example, the little girl you're watching may be extra cranky and cry until her parents come home. Or maybe, the family didn't leave any snacks and you have to starve all night. Even worse, the child could fall and get hurt. Then you have to decide whether you can take care of her yourself or you need to call for help. No, babysitting isn't easy.

Directions: Write the rest of the paragraph for each topic sentence below, using examples to explain what you mean.
1. If the topic sentence gives a choice, select one.
2. Write your examples on another sheet of paper.
3. Read them over and put them in order.
4. When the sentences are the way you want them, copy them below.

Sometimes dreams can be scary.

_____
_____
_____
_____
_____
_____

You can learn a lot by living in a foreign country.

_____
_____
_____
_____
_____
_____

Making Nouns Possessive

A possessive noun owns something.

To make a singular noun possessive, add an apostrophe and **s**:
    mayor**'s** campaign.

To make a plural noun possessive when it already ends with **s**, just add an apostrophe:
    dogs**'** tails.

To make a plural noun possessive when it doesn't end with **s**, add an apostrophe and **s**:
    men**'s** shirts.

Directions: Write in the correct form of the word given for each sentence in that group. Be careful, though. Sometimes the word will need to be singular, sometimes plural, sometimes singular possessive, and sometimes plural possessive.

Like this: **teacher**

How many _____teachers_____ does your school have?

Where is the _____teacher's_____ coat?

All the _____teachers'_____ mailboxes are in the school office.

1. **reporter**

    Two _____ were assigned to the story.

    One _____ car broke down on the way to the scene.

    The other _____ was riding in the car, which had to be towed away.

    Both _____ notes ended up missing.

2. **child**

    The _____ are hungry.

    How much spaghetti can one _____ eat?

    Put this much on each _____ plate.

    The _____ spaghetti is ready for them.

3. **mouse**

    Some _____ made a nest under those boards.

    I can see the _____ hole from here.

    A baby _____ has wandered away from the nest.

    The _____ mother is coming to get it.

Name: _____

Review

Directions: See if you can complete these exercises without looking back at the previous lessons.

1. Write two words with a silent **l**.

_____

2. Write two words with a silent **n**.

_____

3. Write two words with a silent **g**.

_____

4. Write a word with a silent **b** and one with a silent **h**.

_____

5. Write a paragraph that explains why insects can be a nuisance at a picnic. Include several examples of how they can get in the way. First, write your paragraph on another sheet of paper. Then make any needed changes, be sure your topic sentence is first, and copy your paragraph below.

_____

_____

_____

_____

6. Finish this analogy, using a word with a silent **l**:

Fly is to **eagle** as **swim** is to_____.

7. Write a sentence with a plural subject and a plural verb and include the word solemn.

_____

_____

8. Write a sentence with a plural possessive noun and include the word foreign.

_____

_____

9. Find four misspelled words below and write them correctly.
   The teacher wrote the words for a hym on the board with chak. She assined me to clap the rhythem while the others sang.

_____

Name: _____

Using Suffixes, Part I

Some suffixes make nouns into adjectives.
   Like this: fool—foolish; nation—national.

Other suffixes change adjectives into adverbs.
   Like this: foolish—foolishly; national—nationally.

As you can see, a word can have more than one suffix.

Directions: Use the words from the word box in these exercises.

personal	stylish	obviously	professional	typical
childish	practical	medical	permanently	ticklish
additional	critical	gradually	physical	musical

1. Write each word by the word from the same word family.

tickle _____   adding _____   criticism _____

medicine _____   permanent_____   typically _____

person _____   musician _____   children _____

style _____   grade _____   obvious _____

practice _____   profession _____   physician _____

2. In each sentence, circle the word or group of words that is a synonym for a word from the word box. Write the synonym from the word box on the line. The first one is done for you.

Knowing how to cook is a (useful) skill.   _____practical_____

The lake slowly warmed up.   _____

Clearly, I should have stayed on the path.   _____

That is a fashionable outfit.   _____

Wanting your own way all the time is for little kids.   _____

Getting lost is common for me.   _____

My grades are a private matter.   _____

Name: _____

Describing Events In Order

When we write to explain what happened, we need to describe the events in the same order they happened. Words and phrases such as **at first**, **then**, **after that**, and **finally** help us tell the order of events.

Directions: Rewrite the paragraph below, putting the topic sentence first and arranging the events in order. Underline the topic sentence.

I got dressed, but I didn't really feel like eating breakfast. By the time I got to school, my head felt hot so I went to the nurse. This day was terrible from the very beginning. Finally, I ended up where I started, back in my own bed. Then she sent me home again! I just had some toast and left for school. When I first woke up in the morning, my stomach hurt.

_____

_____

_____

_____

_____

_____

Directions: Now write a paragraph telling what happened the last time you tried to cook something—or the last time you tried to fix something that was broken.

1. Write your first draft on another sheet of paper. Start with a topic sentence and add support sentences to explain what happened. Include these phrases to help keep things in order: at first, but then, in the middle of it, at last.
2. Read the paragraph out loud to see if it reads smoothly. Make sure the events are in the right order.
3. Make any needed changes and copy your paragraph below.

_____

_____

_____

_____

_____

_____

Name: _____

Adding The Word To The Suffix

Directions: Add the beginning of the words to their suffixes. Each word from the word box is used once.

personal	stylish	obviously	professional	typical
childish	practical	medical	permanently	ticklish
additional	critical	gradually	physical	musical

1. That's none of your business! Don't ask _____ al questions!

2. Tell me what you do on an ordinary, _____ ical day.

3. He hurt my feelings when he was so _____ ical.

4. My dad needs to get more _____ ical exercise.

5. My brother brings a little more stuff home every day and is _____ ally taking over our whole bedroom.

6. That plan is too expensive. We need to think of something more _____ ical.

7. I want to play the piano, but I don't have any _____ ical talent.

8. Don't touch my feet! I am _____ ish!

9. If you keep making faces, your mouth will stay that way _____ ly.

10. Do you have some shoes that are more up-to-date and _____ ish?

11. Kenny keeps pulling my hair. He is so _____ ish!

12. Are you bleeding? Is this a _____ ical emergency?

13. If there is one more person, we need an _____ al chair.

14. Jenny would like to be a _____ al basketball player.

15. You have _____ ly been working very hard.

Name: _____

Explaining What Happened

Directions: These pictures tell a story, but they're out of order.
Follow these steps to write what happened:

1. On another sheet of paper, write a sentence explaining what is happening in each picture.
2. Put your sentences in order and write a topic sentence.
3. Read the whole paragraph to yourself and add words like **first** and **then** to help show the order in which things happened. Include adjectives and adverbs, maybe even a simile or metaphor, to make your story more interesting.
4. Copy your paragraph below. Be sure to give it a title.

_____

_____

_____

_____

_____

_____

_____

_____

_____

_____

_____

_____

_____

_____

_____

_____

_____

_____

Name: _____

Comparing With Adjectives

When we use adjectives to compare two things:
   With most one-syllable words and some two-syllable words, we add **-er**.
   For example, today is cold**er** than yesterday.

   With many two-syllable words and all words with three or more syllables, we use the word **more** with the adjective.
   For example, Dr. X is **more** professional than Dr. Y.

When we compare three or more things:
   With most one-syllable and some two-syllable words, we add **-est**.
   For example, This is the cold**est** day of the year.

   With longer words, we use **most**.
   For example, Dr. X is the **most** professional doctor in town.

When we're adding **-er** or **-est** to the shorter words, the spelling rules for verbs apply:
   Double the last consonant if the word has a short vowel (thin**ner**),
   Change **y** to **i** before adding an ending (earl**iest**), and
   Drop the final **e** before adding an ending (simpl**er**).

Directions: Finish these sentences with the correct form of the word. Sometimes you will be adding **more** or **most** to the word.

1. This book is (small) _____ than that one.

2. I want the (small) _____ book in the library.

3. My plan is (practical) _____ than yours.

4. My plan is the (practical) _____ one in the class.

5. I wish the change was (gradual) _____ than it is.

6. My sister is the (childish) _____ girl in her day care group.

7. Chris has always been (musical) _____ than I am.

8. There must be a (simple) _____ way to do it than that.

9. This is the (simple) _____ way of the four we thought of.

10. I think your new hair cut is (stylish) _____ than your old one.

11. Is Jon (critical) _____ than Beth?

39

Name: _____

Writing Directions

Directions must be clearly written. They are easiest to follow when they are in numbered steps. Each direction should start with a verb, like these:

How to peel a banana
1. Hold the banana by the stem end.
2. Find a loose edge of peel at the top.
3. Pull the peel down.
4. Peel the other sections of the banana in the same way.

Directions: Rewrite these directions so the steps are in order, are numbered, and start with verbs.

How to feed a dog

Finally, call the dog to come and eat. Then you carry the filled dish to the place where the dog eats. The can or bag should be opened by you. First, clean the dog's food dish with soap and water. Then get the dogfood out of the cupboard. Put the right amount of food in the dish.

_____

_____

_____

_____

_____

_____

Directions:

1. On another sheet of paper, draw two symbols, such as a square with a star in one corner or a triangle inside a circle. Don't show your drawing to anybody.

2. On a different sheet of paper, write instructions that someone else could follow to make the same drawing. Make sure your instructions are clear, in order, numbered, and start with verbs.

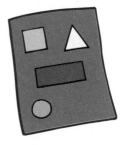

3. Trade instructions (but not pictures) with a partner. See if you can follow each other's instructions to make the drawings.

4. Show your partner the drawing you made in step one. Does it look like the one he or she made following your instructions? Could you follow your partner's instructions? Share what was clear—or not so clear—about each other's instructions.

Name: _____

Finding The Spelling Mistakes

Directions: Find six mistakes in each paragraph and write the words correctly below. Watch for spelling errors, homophones, and problems in the possessive form of nouns. If you need help with spelling, look on pages 11, 19, 27, or 35.

My brother Jim took a math coarse at the high school that was too hard for hymn. My father didn't want him to take it, but Jim said, "Oh, you're just too critcal, Dad. Oviously, you don't think I can do it." Jim ingored Dad. That's norml at our house.

_____ _____ _____

_____ _____ _____

Well, the first day Jim went to the course, he came home with a solem expresion on his face, like a condemed man. "That teacher assined us five pages of homework!" he said. "And two addtional problems that we have to reserch!"

_____ _____ _____

_____ _____ _____

"He sounds like an excelent, profesional teacher," my dad said. "We need more teachers of that qwality in our schools." Jim squirmed in his seat. Then he gradualy started to smile. "Dad, I need some help with a personl problem," he said. "Five pages of problems, right?" Dad asked. Jim just smiled and handed Dad his math book. That's tipical at our house, too.

_____ _____ _____

_____ _____ _____

One day we had a meddical emergensy at home. My sisters' hand got stuck in a basket with a narrow opening, and she couldn't pull it out. I thought she would have to wear the basket on her hand permanentally! First I tried to stretch and exxpand the baskets opening, but that didn't work.

_____ _____ _____

_____ _____ _____

Then I smeared a quanity of butter on my sisters hand and she pulled it right out. I thought she would have the curtesy to thank me, but she just stomped away, still mad. How childsh! Sometimes she seems to think I exxist just to serve her. There are importanter things in the world than her happiness! (My happiness, for example!)

_____ _____ _____

_____ _____ _____

Name: _____

Review

Directions: See if you can complete these exercises without looking back at the previous lessons.

1. Add suffixes to change these words into adjectives.

person_____   music _____   child _____

2. Add suffixes to change these words into adverbs.

permanent_____   obvious _____   gradual _____

3. Write three more words or phrases that help show the order in which events happened.

At first,_____

4. Write a paragraph that tells what you usually do during the first hour after you get up on a school day. Begin with a topic sentence and add support sentences that tell the events in order. Write the first draft of your paragraph on another sheet of paper. Read it to yourself, make any necessary changes, and then copy it below.

_____

_____

_____

_____

5. Write directions that explain how to brush your teeth. You should have at least four steps. Make them as clear as possible and remember to start each one with a verb. (Write a rough draft on another sheet of paper first.)

1. _____

2. _____

3. _____

4. _____

6. On another sheet of paper, write one or two sentences that include at least four of the words below. Misspell the words and see if someone else can find the mistakes and write the words correctly.

personal	stylish	obviously	professional	typical
childish	practical	medical	permanently	ticklish
additional	critical	gradually	physical	musical

Name: _____

Using Suffixes, Part II

The suffixes in these next lessons, **-ion**, **-tion**, and **-ation**, change verbs into nouns.
Thus, **imitate** becomes **imitation**, and **combine** becomes **combination**.

Directions: Use words from the word box in these exercises.

celebration	solution	imitation	exploration	reflection
conversation	population	invitation	combination	decoration
appreciation	definition	selection	suggestion	transportation

1. Write each word from the word box by its definition.

a copy _____   choices _____   talking _____

a party _____   a request _____   the answer _____

the meaning _____   people _____   a search _____

a joining _____   mirror image _____   new idea _____

cars, trucks _____   thankfulness _____   ornaments _____

2. Write the correct forms of each word in the sentences.

Like this:

transport   How are we ____transporting____ our project to school?

     Did anyone arrange ____transportation____ ?

decorate   Yesterday we _____ the classroom.

     We brought the _____ from home.

solve   Have you _____ the problem yet?

     We need a _____ by the end of the day.

suggest   What do you _____ ?

     We haven't heard any _____ from you yet.

appreciate   I really _____ what you did.

     How can I show my _____ ?

define   Please _____ the next word.

     Write the _____ on the board.

imitate   Watch how Steve _____ a dog.

     Steve, do your dog _____ .

Name: _____

Writing From Different Points Of View

A **fact** is a statement that can be proved. An **opinion** is what someone thinks or believes. A **point of view** is one person's opinion about something.

Directions: Follow the instructions below.

1. Write **F** by the facts below and **O** by the opinions.

_____ The amusement park near our town just opened last summer.

_____ It's the best one in our state.

_____ It has a roller coaster that's 300 feet high.

_____ You're a chicken if you don't go on it.

2. Think about the last movie or TV show you saw. Write two facts and two opinions about it.

Facts:

1. _____

2. _____

Opinions:

1. _____

2. _____

3. Pretend you go to the mall with a friend and see a tape you really want on sale. You didn't bring any money, so you borrow five dollars from your friend to buy the tape. Then you lose the money in the store! Write a paragraph describing what happened from the point of view of each person named below. Be sure to explain how each person feels.

Yourself _____

_____

_____

Your friend _____

_____

_____

The store clerk who watches you look for the money _____

_____

_____

The person who finds the money _____

_____

_____

Rhyming Riddles

The answers to rhyming riddles are two four-syllable words.
Here's one: What do you call a pretend party?
(an imitation celebration!)

Directions: Follow the steps below to write rhyming riddles.

1. Write the ten words from the word box that have four syllables.

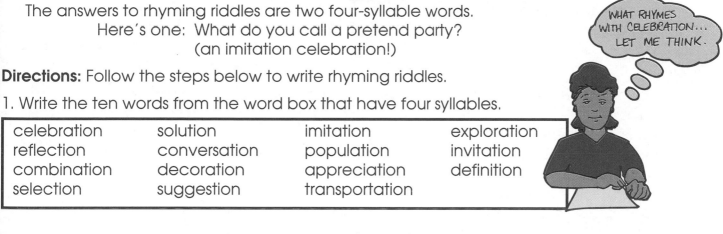

celebration	solution	imitation	exploration
reflection	conversation	population	invitation
combination	decoration	appreciation	definition
selection	suggestion	transportation	

_____

_____

_____

2. For practice, find the answers to these rhyming riddles in the list of words you just wrote.
   Write your answers on the lines.

What do you call carrying a box of bows in from the car?

_____

What do you call talking about how you look in the mirror?

_____

What do you call a group of people who always like our answers?

_____

What do you call searching for the meaning of life?

_____

3. Now, so you have more words to choose from, write five more words that have four
   syllables and end with the suffixes **-ion**, **-tion**, or **-ation**. (Look in the dictionary if you need
   help.)

_____

4. You're ready to write your own riddles now. Write three of them and see if someone else
   can figure out the answers.

1. _____

2. _____

3. _____

Name: _____

Writing Persuasively

When you write to persuade someone, you try to convince the reader that your opinion is correct. "Because I said so" isn't very convincing. Instead, you need to offer as many reasons and facts as possible to support your opinion. It helps to be able to look at both sides of the question.

Directions: To practice being persuasive, write two paragraphs, one persuading the reader that airplanes are better transportation than trains and one persuading the reader that trains are better. Follow these steps:

1. First, on another sheet of paper, list three or four reasons why planes are better and three or four reasons why trains are better.
2. Put each list of reasons in order. (Often persuasive writing is strongest when the best reason is placed last. Readers tend to remember the last reason best.)
3. Write topic sentences for each paragraph.
4. Read each paragraph all the way through, and make any necessary changes so one sentence leads smoothly to the next.
5. Copy your paragraphs below.

Airplanes Are Better Transportation Than Trains

_____

_____

_____

_____

Trains Are Better Transportation Than Planes

_____

_____

_____

_____

6. Now, trade workbooks with a partner. Read his or her paragraphs and decide which one is more convincing. Did your partner persuade you trains are better or planes are better? Why is one paragraph more persuasive than the other? Maybe one is easier to understand. Maybe your partner named reasons for trains (or planes) that you think are true, too. Write your opinion of your partner's paragraphs below.

_____

_____

_____

_____

Writing Stronger Sentences

Sometimes the noun form of a word is not the best way to express an idea.
Compare these two sentences:
They made **preparations** for the party.
They **prepared** for the party.
The second sentence, using **prepared** as a verb instead of a noun, is shorter and stronger.

Directions: In these sentences, write in one word to take the place of a whole phrase. Cross out the words you don't need. The first one is done for you.

1. She ~~made a suggestion~~ suggested that we go on Monday.

2. They arranged decorations around the room.

3. Let's make a combination of the two ideas.

4. I have great appreciation for what you did.

5. The buses are acting as transportation for the classes.

6. The group made an exploration of the Arctic Circle.

7. Please make a selection of one quickly.

8. The lake is making a reflection of the trees.

9. The family had a celebration of the holiday.

10. Would you please provide a solution for this problem?

11. Don made an imitation of his cat.

12. Please give a definition of that word.

13. I made an examination of the broken bike.

14. Stan made an invitation for us to join him.

Name: _____

Considering Point Of View To Persuade

If you made cookies to sell at a school fair, which of these sentences would you write on your sign?

I spent a lot of time making these cookies.

These cookies taste delicious!

If you were writing to ask your school board to start a gynmastics program, which sentence would be more persuasive?

I really am interested in gymnastics.

Gymnastics would be good for our school because both boys and girls can participate, and it's a year-round sport we can do in any weather.

In both situations, the second sentence is more persuasive because it is written from the reader's point of view. People care how the cookies taste, not how long it took you to make them. The school board wants to provide activities for all the students, not just you. Our writing is usually more persuasive if we write from the reader's point of view.

Directions: Mark each item below **R** if it's written from the reader's point of view or **W** if it's written from the writer's point of view.

_____ 1. If you come swimming with me, you'll be able to cool off.

_____ 2. Come swimming with me. I don't want to go alone.

_____ 3. Please write me a letter. I really like to get mail.

_____ 4. Please write me a letter. I want to hear from you.

Directions: On your own paper, write an "invitation," persuading people to move to your town or city. Follow these steps:

1. Think about reasons someone would want to live in your town. Make a list all the good things there, like the schools, parks, annual parades, historic buildings, businesses where parents could work, scout groups, Little League, and so on. You might also describe your town's population, transportation, celebrations, or even holiday decorations.

2. Now select three or four items from your list. On another sheet of paper, write a sentence (or two) about each one from the reader's point of view. For example, instead of writing "Our Little League team won the championship last year," you could tell the reader, "You could help our Little League team win the championship again this year."

3. Write a topic sentence to begin your invitation and put your support sentences in order after it.

4. Read your invitation out loud to a partner. Make any needed changes and copy it on a clean sheet of paper. Perhaps your teacher will post all the invitations on a bulletin board titled "Come to Our Town!"

Using Different Forms Of Words

Directions: Write a sentence for each word
below, using the form given.
Make any necessary spelling changes.

Like this:

live + ing   _Where are you living now?_

explain + tion   _Let me tell you my explanation._

1. solve + tion   _____

2. appreciate + ed   _____

3. define + tion   _____

4. select + ing   _____

5. suggest + ion   _____

6. imitate + ed   _____

7. invite + ing   _____

8. explore + ation   _____

9. combine + ed   _____

10. decorate + ing   _____

11. converse + ation   _____

12. celebrate + ed   _____

13. transport + ing   _____

14. populate + ion   _____

15. suggest + ed   _____

Name: _____

Review

Directions: Can you complete this page correctly without looking back at the previous lessons?

1. Add suffixes to make the noun forms of these verbs:
   select, imitate, invite, decorate, reflect.

_____

_____

2. Write a fact and an opinion about your math class.

Fact:

_____

Opinion:

_____

3. Pretend your neighbor has a dog that barks all night and keeps you awake. Write two or three sentences about the situation from your own point of view and two or three from your neighbor's point of view.

Your point of view: _____

_____

_____

Your neighbor's point of view:_____

_____

_____

4. Write the two-word answer to these rhyming riddles:

What do you call a discussion
about whether the class will ride in
a bus or cars for your next field trip?   _____

What do you call having a party for
Valentine's Day and someone's
birthday on the same day?   _____

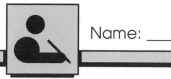

Name: _____

Using Suffixes, Part III

You already learned how some suffixes change verbs into nouns. The suffixes in these next lessons also change verbs (and some adjectives) into nouns. These suffixes are **-ment** as in treatment and **-ity** as in ability.

Directions: In each sentence, circle the word or group of words that is a synonym for a word from the word box. Write the synonym from the word box on the line. Each word from the word box is used once. (Hint: two words from the word box are synonyms for each other.)

equipment	responsibility	activity	curiosity
accomplishment	adjustment	ability	treatment
assignment	personality	achievement	appointment
popularity	astonishment	advertisement	

1. The workers are bringing in their machines. _____

2. What are the duties of this job? _____

3. Do you know our homework for tonight? _____

4. I could see the surprise in his face. _____

5. Do you have a time to see the doctor? _____

6. I was filled with wondering. _____

7. She lists one achievement in particular. _____

8. Look at the exercise on page 16. _____

9. The way you get along with others is part of your character. _____

10. I heard that commercial a hundred times. _____

11. Amy has a strong athletic skill. _____

12. Jason's kindness led to his acceptance by his friends. _____

13. I need to make a change in my schedule. _____

14. That is quite an accomplishment! _____

15. The doctor is trying another way of helping my allergies. _____

Name: _____

Describing Characters In A Story

When you are writing a story, your characters must seem like real people. You need to know not only how they look, but how they act, what they like, and what they're afraid of.

Once you decide what kind of characters are in your story, you need to let the reader know. You could just tell the reader that a character is friendly, scared, or angry, but your story will be more interesting if you show these feelings by the characters' actions.

Directions: Write adjectives, adverbs, similes, and/or metaphors that tell how each character feels. Then write a sentence that shows how the character feels.

Like this: A frightened child _____

            Adjectives and adverbs: _____ scared, lost, worried _____

            Action: _____ He peeked around to see whether anyone was following him.

1. an angry woman

Adjectives and adverbs: _____

Action: _____

2. a disappointed man

Adjectives and adverbs: _____

Action: _____

3. a hungry child

Adjectives and adverbs: _____

Action: _____

4. a tired boy

Adjectives and adverbs: _____

Action: _____

5. a worried girl

Adjectives and adverbs: _____

Action: _____

6. a sick child

Adjectives and adverbs: _____

Action: _____

Name: _____

Finishing Analogies

Directions: In each analogy below, look at the relationship between the first pair of words. Then finish the analogy with the correct form of the word in the second pair. (In these analogies you won't be concerned about synonyms or opposites, just the form of the words.) The word box will help you with spelling.

equipment	responsibility	activity	curiosity	accomplishment
adjustment	ability	treatment	assignment	personality
achievement	appointment	popularity	astonishment	advertisement

Like this: **Decorate** is to **decoration** as **prevent** is to _____ .

1. **Appoint** is to **appointment** as **equip** is to _____ .

2. **Curious** is to **curiosity** as **personal** is to _____ .

3. **Improve** is to **improvement** as **treat** is to _____ .

4. **Possible** is to **possibility** as **active** is to _____ .

5. **Resign** is to **resignation** as **assign** is to _____ .

6. **Prepare** is to **preparation** as **accomplish** is to _____ .

7. **Injure** is to **injury** as **advertise** is to _____ .

8. **Laugh** is to **laughter** as **appoint** is to _____ .

9. **Childish** is to **child** as **able** is to _____ .

10. **Free** is to **freedom** as **popular** is to _____ .

11. **Combine** is to **combination** as **adjust** is to _____ .

12. **Capable** is to **capability** as **curious** is to _____ .

13. **Beautiful** is to **beauty** as **responsible** is to _____ .

14. **Reflect** is to **reflection** as **astonish** is to _____ .

15. **Explore** is to **exploration** as **appoint** is to _____ .

16. **Achieve** is to **achieving** as **adjust** is to _____ .

17. **Definition** is to **define** as **assignment** is to _____ .

18. **Equip** is to **equipped** as **advertise** is to _____ .

19. **Scare** is to **scared** as **astonish** is to _____ .

20. **Accomplish** is to **accomplishing** as **treat** is to _____ .

Name: _____

Setting The Scene For A Story

Where and when a story takes place is called a setting.

As with characters, you can **tell** about a setting—or you can **show** what the setting is like.

Compare these two pairs of sentences:

The sun was shining.
The brightness of the sun made my eyes burn.

The bus was crowded.
Paige pushed down the aisle, searching for an empty seat.

If you give your readers a clear picture of your story's setting, they'll feel as if they're standing beside your characters.

Directions: Think about what each setting below might look, sound, feel, and even smell like. Then write at least two sentences for each setting, clearly describing it for your readers.

1. an empty kitchen early in the morning

_____

_____

_____

2. a locker room after a basketball game

_____

_____

_____

3. a dark living room during a scary TV movie

_____

_____

_____

4. a classroom on the first day of school

_____

_____

_____

5. a quiet place in the woods

_____

_____

_____

Name: _____

Crossing Words

Directions: Read each definition. Write the word that is defined in the spaces that start with the same number. If you need help with spelling, look in the word box on page 51.

Across

1. Having lots of friends
4. Whether you're cheerful or grouchy
7. Moving around
8. A skill
10. Work to do in class or at home
11. What you need before you can do a project
12. Wondering about something

Down

2. Having to be somewhere at a certain time
3. What you feel when you're surprised
5. Something else you've done
6. A change
9. How the doctor helps you get better

Name: _____

Figuring Out A Plot

THE BUTLER DID IT.

When you're writing a story, the **plot** is the problem your characters face and how they solve it. In the beginning of the story, you introduce the characters, setting, and problem. In the middle of the story, your characters try different ways to solve the problem, usually failing at first. In the end, the characters find a way to solve the problem. In some stories, they decide they can live with the situation the way it is.

Here's one plot:

On the way home from school, Scott and Cindy talk together and let us know they live with their grandmother and father. Their mother, whom they've never seen, lives in another state. Then they notice a car following them. They hurry home and tell their grandmother, but she thinks it's their imagination. They tell their father, but he's fixing the washer and not really listening. The next day after school the car is there again.

The car follows them for several days, even when they walk home different ways. No one gets out of the car or talks to them. The windshield is tinted, so they can't see who's driving. Their grandmother still doesn't believe them; she thinks they watch too much TV. The father asks why anyone would follow them.

Finally the kids take a new way home and end up trapped in an alley, blocked in by the car. Just as the car door opens and a man starts to get out, they find a way out of the alley.

How do you think this story ends?

Directions: Now write your own plot, following these steps. Use your own paper.

1. Pick one or two of the characters you described on page 52 (or different ones) and a setting from page 54 (or a different one).
2. Think about how these characters would know each other.
   Are they related? Are they neighbors?
3. What kinds of problems might they face? Jot your ideas on scratch paper.
4. Pick a problem and think of ways the characters might try to solve it. Put the ways in order, with the solution that works last.
5. Add more details. Then write your plot outline on another sheet of paper.
6. Now write the whole story on another sheet of paper. You don't need to follow your plot outline if you think of a better idea. Make your story exciting!
7. Read your story out loud to yourself. Is what happened clear?
8. Make any needed changes and rewrite your story.
9. Trade stories with a partner. Tell your partner what you like about his or her story.

Name: _____

Using Suffixes In Sentences

Directions: Finish each sentence by adding one (or two) of the suffixes or word endings below to the word given. Be sure to use the correct form of the word.

-ed	-ing	-ly	-al	-ish	-ion	-tion	-ation	-ment	-ity

ED ING AL LY ION

Like this: **person**   I _____personally_____ asked him to come.

equip   1. We need more _____ for our trip.

adjust   2. My sister is _____ the handles for me.

popular   3. That singer's _____ is amazing.

advertise   4. Did you see the _____ ?

imitate   5. I think that diamond is an _____ .

child   6. My little cousin is so _____ .

add   7. We need two _____ people for our play.

astonish   8. He was _____ by the turnout.

decorate   9. Do you like our _____ ?

responsible   10. Will you take the _____ by yourself?

appoint   11. We were _____ to take care of it.

achieve   12. Did you see the list of her _____ ?

accomplish   13. She is _____ the impossible.

able   14. I didn't know she had all that _____ .

curious   15. I am _____ waiting for her answer.

invite   16. He already _____ her to come.

suggest   17. My _____ is still a good one.

solve   18. I guess that _____ the problem.

select   19. Did you make a _____ ?

active   20. Which _____ did you select?

Name: _____

Review

Directions: Complete these exercises to show what you've learned in the previous lessons.

1. Write the noun form of these words: curious, accomplish, adjust, treat, assign.

_____

2. Describe the actions of a story character your age. Show that he or she is friendly.

_____

_____

3. Write a description of a story setting of your choice. Appeal to at least two of the reader's senses (sight, hearing, touch, smell, taste).

_____

_____

_____

4. Write at least one problem the character you described in #2 might face in the setting you described in #3. What are at least two ways the character might try to solve that problem?

_____

_____

_____

_____

5. Find four misspelled words in each paragraph and write them correctly on the lines.

It was Alysha's responsibity to bring in the equippment after gym class. Actually, it was quite an acomplishment to find all the volley balls. I never managed that acheivement myself.

_____ _____ _____ _____ _____

Some kind of weird activty was going on in a little room off our science classroom. I was filled with curosity to find out what it was. One day I had an apointment with the science teacher to talk about an assinement. I hoped I'd get to go in the little room.

_____ _____ _____ _____ _____

Imagine my astonishement when the teacher asked me to go in the little room and make an "ajustment," as he called it. A big box in the room had a sign that said "Do not open." Well, you know me. When the teacher wasn't looking, I opened it. An alarm went off! I turned to see the teacher smiling at me. It turns out it was a personity test to check my abilty to resist temptation!

_____ _____ _____ _____ _____

Name: _____

Using Prefixes

A prefix is a syllable added to the beginning of a word to change its meaning.

The prefix **re-** means "back or again," as in **re**turn.

Pre- means "before," as in **pre**pare.

Dis- means "do the opposite," as in **dis**appear.

In- and **im-** both can mean "not," as in **im**possible.
(These two prefixes also have other meanings.)

Com- and **con-** both mean "with," as in **com**panion and **con**cert.

Here's a rule to help you know whether to use **im-** or **in-** and whether to use **com-** or **con-**:

Use **im-** and **com-** before syllables that start with /**p**/, /**b**/,or /**m**/.
(You say /**p**/, /**b**/, and /**m**/ by pushing your lips together, making it easier to say **im-** and **com-**.)

Use **in-** and **con-** before syllables that start with a vowel or other consonants.

Directions: Use words from the word box in these exercises.

discourage	recite	comparison	impolite	previous
impatient	distrust	conference	prevent	incomplete
invisible	dislike	confide	communicate	recover

1. Match each word from the word box to its definition.

share ideas _____   meeting _____

not finished _____   hate _____

looking for sameness _____   former _____

become normal again _____   rude _____

take away confidence _____   stop _____

in a hurry _____   doubt _____

tell secrets _____   not seen _____

say from memory _____

2. Add the rest of the word to each prefix in these sentences. Use each word from the word box only once.

When he con_____ why he felt dis_____ , I tried to help him gain some confidence.

She seemed hurried and im_____ during our con_____ .

I'd like to re_____ that poem, but my memory of it is in_____ .

I used to dis_____ poetry, but now nothing can pre_____ me from reading it.

Name: _____

Learning To Write Dialogue

Your stories will be more interesting if your characters talk to each other. Conversations help show the characters' feelings and personalities. Compare these two scenes from a story:

Chad asked Angela to help him with his homework. She said she wouldn't because she was mad at him for flirting with Nicole.

"Angela, would you be a real friend and help me with this math problem?" Chad asked with a big smile. "I'm awfully busy, Chad," Angela answered without looking up." Maybe you should ask Nicole since you like to talk to her so much."

In the second version, we know Angela is angry even though the writer didn't use that word. In the same way, you can show how your characters feel by what they say and how they say it.

When you write dialogue, remember to start a new paragraph every time a different person talks. Also, don't forget to put quotation marks around the words the person says. Commas and periods at the ends of sentences go inside the quotation marks.

Directions: Pretend you're writing a story. In your story, the teacher has just explained a new assignment the class will do in groups. The bell rings and everyone heads for the lunchroom. Write what each character below might say to a classmate. Use dialogue to show how each person is feeling without mentioning the name of the feeling ("discouraged" and so on). Include another person in each dialogue. (Use more paper if you need it.)

1. A discouraged girl who isn't sure she can do the project

2. A self-confident boy who got an A on the last project

3. An impatient girl who has an idea and wants to get started

4. An angry boy who dislikes group projects

5. A bored girl who doesn't care about the project

6. A boy who is worried about a different problem in his life

_____

_____

_____

_____

_____

_____

Name: _____

Using Suffixes And Prefixes

Directions: Write each word from the word box by one below from the same word family.

discourage	recite	comparison	impolite	previous
impatient	distrust	conference	prevent	incomplete
invisible	dislike	confide	communicate	recover

vision _____

courage _____

obvious _____

discover _____

compare _____

patience _____

likable _____

recital _____

confidence _____

politely _____

prevention _____

confer _____

completely _____

trusting _____

communication _____

Directions: Add and subtract suffixes and prefixes to make new words. Some of the new words are from the word box.

1. patiently - -ly + im- = _____

2. discourage - dis- + en- + -ment = _____

3. visible + in- = _____

4. likely - -ly + dis- = _____

5. invent - in- + pre- = _____

6. recover - re- + un = _____

7. completion - -ion + in- = _____

8. dislike - dis- + un- = _____

HEY, WE'RE FROM THE SAME WORD FAMILY!

WORD   ANOTHER WORD

Directions: Finish each sentence with the correct form of the word given.

communicate   1. The TV station is _____ news bulletins.

discourage   2. My grade on that test was _____ .

distrust   3. I _____ him from the beginning.

Name: _____

Writing Dialogue In Stories

Directions: Rewrite each paragraph below except the first one. Explain the same scenes and the same feelings with dialogue. Try to write dialogue that sounds natural, the way people really talk. To get started, read the example at the top of page 60 again.

When it was Megan's turn to present her book report to the class, she dropped all her notecards! Her face turned red and she wished she were invisible, but all she could do was stand there and say what she could remember without her cards. It was awful!

After class, Megan told her friend Sara she had never been so embarrassed in her life. She saw everyone staring at her and the teacher looked impatient, but there wasn't anything she could do. Sara assured Megan that no one disliked her because of what had happened.

_____

_____

_____

_____

When Megan got home, she told her grandmother about it. By then she felt like crying. Her grandmother said not to get discouraged. In a couple of days, she would be able to laugh about dropping the cards.

_____

_____

_____

_____

When Megan's older brother Jed came home, he asked her what was wrong. She briefly told him and said she never was going back to school. He started laughing. Megan got mad because she thought he was laughing at her. Then Jed explained that he had done almost the same thing when he was in sixth grade. He was really embarrassed, too, but not for long.

_____

_____

_____

_____

Megan thought about her big brother standing in front of his class with his notecards spilled all over the floor the way hers had been. Then she smiled and told Jed it already seemed a little funny and maybe she would go back to school the next day after all.

_____

_____

_____

_____

Name: _____

Finding Spelling Mistakes

Directions: One word in each sentence below is misspelled. Write the word correctly on the line. If you have trouble, look in the word boxes on pages 3, 11, 19, 27, 35, 43, 51, and 59.

FINED THE
SPELLENG
MYSTAKES

1. Jeff felt discoraged at the comparison between him and his older brother.   _____

2. I got inpatient as my curiosity grew.   _____

3. She confided that she had not finished the asignment.   _____

4. They made the selection after a brief conferrence.   _____

5. Obviusly, it's impolite to sneeze on someone.   _____

6. This skin cream is practicaly invisible.   _____

7. What would prevent you from taking on addtional work?   _____

8. I can resite the words to that hymn.   _____

9. In a previous columm, the newspaper explained the situation.   _____

10. He decieved me so many times that now I distrust him.   _____

11. Please have the curtesy to observe the "No Smoking" signs.   _____

12. The advertisement is so small that it's nearly invisble.   _____

13. The best way to communicate is in a face-to-face conservation.   _____

14. In a cost comparson, salmon is more expensive than tuna.   _____

15. Poplarity among friends shouldn't depend on your accomplishments.   _____

16. Her campaign was quite an acheivement.   _____

17. He condemned it as a poor imitation.   _____

Name: _____

Testing Myself

Directions: The exercises below test some of the skills you've learned throughout this workbook. See if you can complete them without looking back at the lessons.

> I CAN HELP YOU OUT.

LEARN TO SPELL

1. Write a word that:

Spells /ā/ with ei _____

Has the /ûr/ sound _____

Has the /kw/ sound _____

Has a silent g _____

2. Use the right form of each word in these sentences, adding prefixes or suffixes:

profession   He wants to be a _____ baseball player.   _____

gradual   My brother is _____ getting taller than me.   _____

combine   What is the _____ to your locker?   _____

assign   Do you know the math _____ ?   _____

curious   _____ can lead to great discoveries.   _____

3. Finish these two sentences in ways that make sense:

I called my friend on the phone because _____

I called my friend on the phone, but _____

4. Finish this sentence with a simile:

The sky was a gloomy as _____

5. Write an acrostic poem (rhymed or unrhymed) for this word: RAIN

_____

_____

_____

_____

Join Us

Do this activity with a family member or friend.
Together, think up a really strange or unusual hobby.
Here are some ideas: collecting lint from clothes dryers, hiking around parking lots, taking pictures of out-of-shape paper clips.
Make up a club or an organization for the hobby.
Here are some examples: Fans of Lint United for Fuzz (FLUFF), White Lines—Parking Lot Hikers Club, Clips Living in Photographs (CLIP).
Then make notes below for a letter or an advertisement inviting people to join the club or organization.

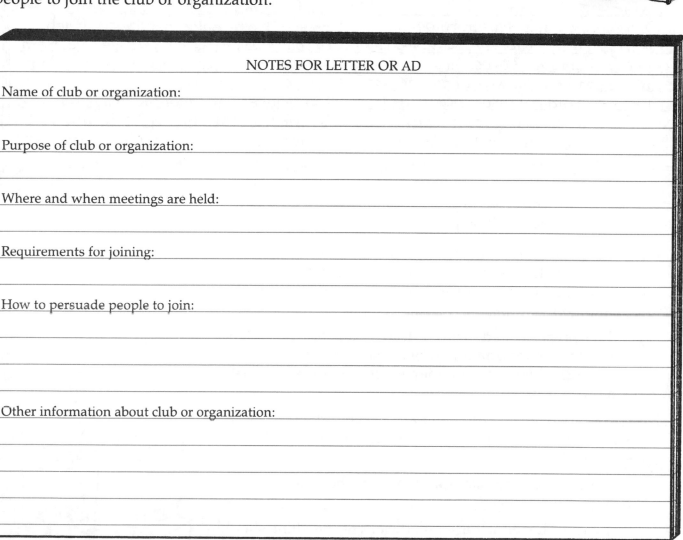

NOTES FOR LETTER OR AD

Name of club or organization:

Purpose of club or organization:

Where and when meetings are held:

Requirements for joining:

How to persuade people to join:

Other information about club or organization:

Now work together to write your letter or ad.
Use the information in your notes and write on separate paper.
Do your best to make people eager to join.
Try to inform, persuade, *and* entertain them.
Take your letter or ad to school and share it with your classmates.
See if they would like to join your club or organization.

News Reporter

Work with a friend on this activity.
Pretend you are reporters who were sent to cover a robbery.
Here are the notes you took at the scene of the crime.
Take a few minutes to review your notes.

Jewelry store broken into.
Stylish Jewelers - 100 High Street.
 Alarm didn't go off.
 Owner - Jody Hardy.
 Discovered early this morning.
Investigated by police-Detective Maria Rao.
$15,000 in diamonds, $25,000 in gold missing.
Burglar seemed to know what to look for.
"I had just paid my insurance and
installed alarms. Why me?" - Hardy
"We don't have a suspect yet, but

officers are combing the store for
fingerprints and other clues". - Rao
 Fifth jewelry store robbery this year.
Hardy blaming police Chief Willy Green.
Green- "We're doing our best. Each
robbery was different. We see no pattern".
Glass broken in small window in rear door.
 No other damage.
Store closed until Monday, maybe longer.
Meanwhile, Hardy hiring 24-hour guard.
Hardy-"I just don't feel safe anymore".

Now you have to write your article for tomorrow's newspaper.
The instructions below will help you.

1. Write the question words *who, what, where, when, why,* and *how*
   down the left side of a sheet of paper. Work together to find
   information in your notes to answer each question. Write the
   information on your paper.

2. A good news article starts with a "lead"—one or two sentences
   that tell the most important part of the story right away.
   Together, work out a lead for your article and write the final
   version on your paper.

3. Now work together to write your article about the jewelry store
   robbery. Start with your lead and include the answers to the
   question words.

4. Review your article and make any changes that are necessary.
   Then make a final copy.

5. Finally, write a headline for your article. The headline should
   be short, get people's attention, and give information. Try to
   use no more than seven words in your headline. Write it at the
   top of your article.

Take your article to school tomorrow.
Get together with some classmates and read your articles to each other.
Decide whose article should be "printed" in the newspaper.

Writing a newspaper article

The Magic Triangle

In ancient Egypt, builders had a special way of making square corners when marking out fields or planning buildings. They used a "magic" triangle made out of a piece of rope.

Ask a friend to do this activity with you.
You and your friend will find out how a magic triangle works.
First, get a long piece of string and make thirteen equally spaced dark marks on it.
Put the two end marks together and tie a knot where they meet.
Cut off any extra string.
Now you have a loop with twelve equal spaces.
It should look something like this. ⟶

Next, look around for something with a square corner.
It could be the corner of a floor tile, table top, book, or box.
Put the knot of your loop at the corner and have your friend hold it down.
Then stretch the loop along the two sides of the corner until all three sides of the string are tight.
Slide your hands along the string, keeping the sides tight, until you have a mark in each hand.
You should have a triangle that looks like this. ⟶

How many spaces—places between marks—are on the sides of your corner? _____ and _____
How many spaces are on the slanted side opposite the corner? _____

Now measure three other things with square corners.
Record the results below.

	NUMBER OF SPACES ON SIDES OF CORNER		NUMBER OF SPACES OPPOSITE CORNER
Item 1			
Item 2			
Item 3			

If you measured correctly, you should have counted three, four, and five spaces every time.
Anytime you have a triangle with the sides in a three, four, five relationship, you have a triangle with one square corner, or a right triangle.
And a right triangle was the magic triangle the ancient Egyptian builders used to make their square corners!

Who Am I?

Play this game with someone your own age.
Have the other player close his or her eyes while you toss a coin
onto the History Board.
Remove the coin and read the name of the person to yourself.
If you land on a person who has already been used, toss again.
Then tell what you know about the person, but do *not* name the person.
Give as much information as you can and ask "Who am I?" at the end.
If the other player can name the person, score 2 points.
If the other player cannot name the person, score 1 point.
If you do not know anything about the person, score 0.
Take turns and play six rounds. Keep score on a piece of paper.
The winner is the player with more points.

History Board

Theodore Roosevelt	Susan B. Anthony	Frederick Douglass	Sacagawea
Harriet Tubman	Daniel Boone	Amelia Earhart	George Washington Carver
Chief Joseph	Elizabeth Blackwell	Benjamin Franklin	Jane Addams
Clara Barton	John Paul Jones	Sojourner Truth	Abraham Lincoln

Dear Diary

A diary is an account, written each day, of the writer's thoughts and experiences that day.

Here are four imaginary diary entries by people who invented some common everyday objects.

Read each entry and complete the sentence at the end.

The answer is one of the objects pictured on this page.

> It occurred to me this morning that there must be an easier way to clean my teeth than with a rag. So I picked out a small bone from a piece of meat and drilled holes in it. Then I tied together some small bunches of short, stiff animal hairs and wedged them into the holes. When I tried it out, it worked like a charm! Why didn't I think of this sooner?
>
> This person invented the _____.

> Success at last! Today I tried out the latest version of my platform to hoist the beds in the factory up and down from one floor to another. The addition of the built-in safety device—to keep the platform from crashing down if the pulley rope breaks—was just what was needed. I will test the platform again, but I think I have finally gotten it right.
>
> This person invented the _____.

> After months of experimenting, I have found the right adhesive to coat the transparent tape I developed for the refrigerator car manufacturers! The new adhesive is very strong and is practically invisible when applied to the tape. Tomorrow I will take some tape with the new adhesive to the refrigerator car people. Hope they'll be pleased.
>
> This person invented _____.

> So many other people have tried to get this machine to work, but I think I have now come up with a way to do it. If I put each letter on an individual bar attached to a keypad, then each letter would hit the paper independently of the others. All you would need to do is push down on the keypads one at a time and they would spell out words. First thing in the morning I will start working on a new model of the machine.
>
> This person invented the _____.

Reading diaries

Finish It for Me

This is an activity for you and a friend.
Begin a realistic or fantasy story below.
Then have your friend finish the story.
If you start a realistic story, your friend should add characters and events to turn it into a fantasy.
If you start a fantasy, your friend should add characters and events to explain away the fantasy.
When your friend is finished, have him or her begin a story. The story may be realistic or fantasy.
Then you add characters and events to change it into the opposite kind of story.
When you are finished, read your stories aloud to each other.

Did I ever tell you about the space monsters disguised as basketballs?

I bet they just had funny faces painted on them.

My beginning: _____

_____

_____

_____

_____

_____

_____

_____

_____

My friend's ending: _____

_____

_____

_____

_____

_____

_____

_____

_____

My friend's beginning: _____

_____

_____

_____

_____

_____

_____

_____

_____

My ending: _____

_____

_____

_____

_____

_____

_____

_____

_____

Writing realistic fiction and fantasy

Fetch!

A play contains a list of characters, some stage directions, and the characters' words.
The whole story is told by what the characters say and do.
Read the play below.
Then answer the questions at the end.

FETCH!

Cast: MARSHA, A TWELVE-YEAR-OLD GIRL   NINA, ANOTHER FRIEND
DELO, MARSHA'S DOG   A TOY HAMSTER
DWAYNE, MARSHA'S BEST FRIEND

Scene 1

(The friends are in DWAYNE'S backyard, which has a picnic table. NINA has brought a cage with a small toy HAMSTER in it. The hamster is connected by a thin black thread to a stagehand off stage. The cage is on the picnic table. DELO is sleeping under the table.)

DWAYNE *(to Marsha)*: When did you get Delo?

MARSHA *(looking fondly at dog under table)*: About a year ago. He was one of those police dogs specially trained to track down things by their smell and bring them back. But he's retired now.

DWAYNE *(sighing)*: I wish I had a dog. But the landlord says no pets allowed unless they live in cages. *(opening door of hamster's cage)* Let's see this hamster you brought me, Nina. *(He picks up the hamster, fumbles, and drops it onto the table.)* Oops! It got away.

NINA: Look out! It's running to the edge of the table. *(She makes a grab for the hamster.)* Oh, no! It's running away!

(All watch as stagehand pulls the hamster off stage.)

1. What is the title of the play? _____

2. How many characters are in the play? _____

3. Where does the action take place? _____

4. What makes the hamster move? _____

_____

5. What do you think will happen next? _____

_____

_____

_____

Understanding a play

71

Radio Play

Here is an activity to do with two or more friends.
There are ideas for a radio play on the radio below.
Together, choose one of the ideas, or use your own idea.
In a radio play, everything that happens is spoken or makes a sound because the audience cannot see the performers.
Most of the story is told by the characters as they talk to each other.
Sometimes there is a narrator who tells or explains what is happening.
Sound effects are also used to help listeners imagine what is happening.
Talk with your friends to plan your radio play.
Make notes below.

Notes for Radio Play

Characters: _____

Setting: _____

Important Events: _____

_____

_____

Outcomes: _____

_____

Now work together to develop your radio play.
On separate paper, write the lines for each character.
Remember to include sound effects and a narrator if you need them to tell your story.
You do not need stage directions. Just have the narrator tell or explain what is happening.
When you are finished writing, choose roles and practice reading your lines and creating the sound effects.
Then gather an audience, such as your family, classmates, or friends, and put on your play.
You may want to stand behind a screen, sheet, or curtain so the audience cannot see you.

Writing a play; creating dialogue

ANSWER KEY

MASTER SPELLING/WRITING
6

Spelling and Writing Name: _____

Spelling Words With ie And ei

Many people have trouble deciding whether to spell a word **ie** or **ei**, with good reason. The following rules have many exceptions, but they may be helpful to you. If the two letters are pronounced /ē/ and are preceded by an /s/ sound, spell them **ei**, as in receive. If the two letters are pronounced /ē/ but are not preceded by an /s/ sound, spell them **ie** as in believe. If the letters are pronounced /ā/, spell them **eigh** as in eight or **ei** as in vein. If the letters are pronounced /ī/, spell them **eigh** then, too, as in height.

Directions: Use the words from the word box in these exercises.

veil	brief	deceive	belief	niece
vein	reindeer	yield	achieve	height
neighbor	seize	grief	ceiling	weight

1. Write each word in the row that names at least one of its vowel sounds. (One word will be listed twice.)

/ē/ _deceive   seize   ceiling_
/ē/ _brief belief niece yield achieve grief reindeer_
/ā/ _veil vein reindeer neighbor weight_
/ī/ _height_

2. Finish each sentence with a word that has the vowel sound given. Use each word from the word box only once.

My next-door /ā/ _neighbor_ wore a long /ā/ _veil_ at her wedding.

Will the roof hold the /ā/ _weight_ of Santa's /ā/ _reindeer_ ?

My nephew and /ē/ _niece_ work hard to /ē/ _achieve_ their goals.

I have a strong /ē/ _belief_ they would never /ē/ _deceive_ me.

For a /ē/ _brief_ moment, I thought I'm would /ē/ _yield_ the game to me.

The blood rushed through my /ā/ _veins_.

What is the /ī/ _height_ of this /ē/ _ceiling_ ?

The thief was going to /ē/ _seize_ the money!

Copyright © 1991 American Education Publishing Co.

3

Spelling and Writing Name: _____

Writing Four Kinds Of Sentences

Remember the four main kinds of sentences:
   A **statement** tells something.
   A **question** asks something.
   A **command** tells someone to do something.
   An **exclamation** shows strong feeling or excitement.

Directions: Write what you would say in each situation below. Then tell whether the sentence you wrote was a statement, question, command, or exclamation. Write at least one of each. Be sure to use periods after statements and commands, question marks after questions, and exclamation marks after exclamations.

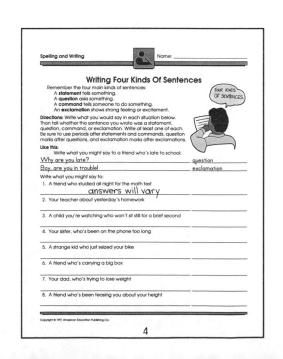

Like this:
   Write what you might say to a friend who's late to school:
Why are you late?   question
Boy, are you in trouble!   exclamation

Write what you might say to:

1. A friend who studied all night for the math test
_____ answers will vary _____

2. Your teacher about yesterday's homework
_____

3. A child you're watching who won't sit still for a brief second
_____

4. Your sister, who's been on the phone too long
_____

5. A strange kid who just seized your bike
_____

6. A friend who's carrying a big box
_____

7. Your dad, who's trying to lose weight
_____

8. A friend who's been teasing you about your height
_____

Copyright © 1991 American Education Publishing Co.

4

Page 5

Figuring Out Homophones

Homophones are two words that sound the same, but have different spellings and different meanings. Here are several homophones: night/knight, fair/fare, not/knot.

Directions: Finish each sentence with the correct homophone. Then write another sentence using the other homophone in the pair.

Like this:

Eight/ate   So far I <u>ate</u> two cookies.

    Joanie had <u>eight</u> cookies!

ATE

EIGHT 8

1. Vein/vain

Since the newspaper printed his picture, Andy has been so self-centered and <u>vain</u>.

<u>varies</u>

2. Weight/wait

We had to <u>wait</u> a long time for the show to start.

<u>varies</u>

3. Weigh/way

He always wants insists that we do it his <u>way</u>.

<u>varies</u>

4. Seize/seas

The explorers charted the <u>seas</u>.

<u>varies</u>

Directions: Write each word from the word box next to the way it's pronounced.

veil	brief	deceive	belief	niece
vein	reindeer	yield	achieve	height
neighbor	seize	grief	ceiling	weight

/bĕlēf/ <u>belief</u>   /sēz/ <u>seize</u>   /nābər/ <u>neighbor</u>

/vāl/ <u>veil</u>   /rāndər/ <u>reindeer</u>   /hīt/ <u>height</u>

/wāt/ <u>weight</u>   /yēld/ <u>yield</u>   /grēf/ <u>grief</u>

/sēling/ <u>ceiling</u>   /dēsēv/ <u>deceive</u>   /brēf/ <u>brief</u>

/achēv/ <u>achieve</u>   /nēs/ <u>niece</u>   /vān/ <u>vein</u>

5

Page 6

Knowing How To Use Sentence Parts

The **subject** tells whom or what a sentence is about.

   Sentences can have more than one subject: Dogs and cats make good pets.

The **verb** tells what the subject does or that it simply "is."

   Verbs can be more than one word: plays, is walking, had been said.

An **adjective** is a word or group of words that describes the subject or another noun.

   For example: cheerful, with blue spots.

An **adverb** is a word or group of words that tells how, when, where, or how often.

   For example: quietly, today, in a tree.

Directions: Mark how each underlined word or group of words is used in these sentences. Write **S** above the subjects, **V** above the verbs, **ADJ** above the adjectives, and **ADV** above the adverbs.

Like this:

   ADJ S   ADJ   V   ADV

   A huge dog with long teeth was barking fiercely.

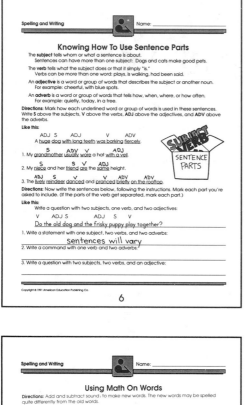

1.   S   ADV   V   ADJ

   My grandmother usually wore a hat with a veil.

2.   S   S   V   ADJ

   My niece and her friend are the same height.

3.   ADJ   S   V   ADV   ADV

   The lively reindeer danced and pranced briefly on the rooftop.

Directions: Now write the sentences below, following the instructions. Mark each part you're asked to include. (If the parts of the verb get separated, mark each part.)

Like this:

   Write a question with two subjects, one verb, and two adjectives:

   V   ADJ   S   ADJ   S   V

   Do the old dog and the frisky puppy play together?

1. Write a statement with one subject, two verbs, and two adverbs:

   <u>sentences will vary</u>

2. Write a command with one verb and two adverbs:

3. Write a question with two subjects, two verbs, and an adjective:

6

Page 7

Using Math On Words

Directions: Add and subtract sounds to make new words. The new words may be spelled quite differently from the old words.

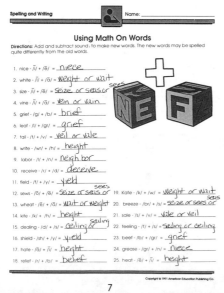

1. nice - /ī/ + /ē/ = <u>niece</u>
2. white - /ī/ + /ā/ = <u>weight or wait</u>
3. size - /ī/ + /ē/ = <u>seize or seas/sees</u>
4. vine - /ī/ + /ā/ = <u>vein or vain</u>
5. grief - /g/ + /b/ = <u>brief</u>
6. leaf - /l/ + /g/ = <u>grief</u>
7. tail - /t/ + /v/ = <u>veil or vale</u>
8. write - /wrt/ + /h/ = <u>height</u>
9. labor - /l/ + /n/ = <u>neighbor</u>
10. receive - /r/ + /d/ = <u>deceive</u>
11. field - /t/ + /y/ = <u>yield</u>
12. sews - /ō/ + /ē/ = <u>seize or seas/sees</u>
13. wheat - /ē/ + /ā/ = <u>wait or weight</u>
14. kite - /k/ + /h/ = <u>height</u>
15. dealing - /d/ + /s/ = <u>ceiling or sealing</u>
16. shield - /sh/ + /y/ = <u>yield</u>
17. hate - /ā/ + /ī/ = <u>height</u>
18. relief - /r/ + /b/ = <u>belief</u>
19. Kate - /k/ + /w/ = <u>weight or wait</u>
20. breeze - /br/ + /s/ = <u>seize or seas/sees or</u>
21. sale - /s/ + /v/ = <u>vale or veil</u>
22. feeling - /f/ + /s/ = <u>sealing or ceiling</u>
23. beet - /b/ + /gr/ = <u>grief</u>
24. grease - /gr/ + /n/ = <u>niece</u>
25. heat - /ē/ + /ī/ = <u>height</u>

7

Page 8

Putting Ideas Together

We join two sentences with **and** when they are more or less equal:

   Julie is coming, **and** she is bringing cookies.

We join two sentences with **but** when the second sentence contradicts the first one:

   Julie is coming, **but** she will be late.

We join two sentences with **or** when they name a choice:

   Julie might bring cookies, **or** she might bring a cake.

We join two sentences with **because** when the second one names the reason for the first one:

   I'll bring cookies, too, **because** Julie might forget hers.

We join two sentences with **so** when the second one names a result of the first one:

   Julie is bringing cookies, **so** we won't starve.

Directions: Finish each sentence with an idea that fits with the first part.

Like this:

   We could watch TV, or <u>we could play Monopoly</u>.

1. I wanted to seize the opportunity, but <u>sentences will vary</u>

2. You had better not deceive me because _____

3. My neighbor was on vacation, so _____

4. Veins take blood back to your heart, and _____

5. You can't always yield to your impulses because _____

6. I know that is your belief, but _____

7. It could be reindeer on the roof, or _____

8. Brent was determined to achieve his goal, so _____

9. Brittany was proud of her height because _____

10. We painted the ceiling, and _____

8

Page 9

Spelling Some Tough Words

Directions: Write in the missing letters in the words below. If you have trouble, look in the word box on page 3.

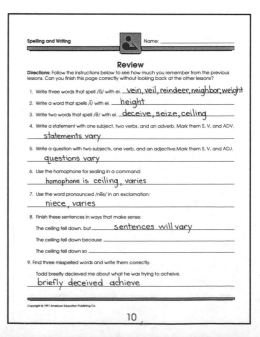

REINDEER: EI, EE, AE, ...

Some people are dec**ei**ved into thinking that r**ei**ndeer aren't real. Actually, r**ei**ndeer live in colder areas of North America and other parts of the world. They reach a h**ei**ght of 2.3-4.6 feet at the shoulder. Their w**ei**ght may be 600 pounds. When the males battle, one of them y**ie**lds to the other.

My n**ei**ghbor had a stroke. One of his v**ei**ns burst in his brain, so now he has trouble walking. Instead of being overcome with gr**ie**f, he exercises every day so he can ach**ie**ve his goal of walking again. I have a strong bel**ie**f that some day soon I will see him walking all by himself.

Directions: Only one word in each sentence below is misspelled. Write it correctly on the line.

1. Fierce wolves hunt the raindeer.   <u>reindeer</u>
2. My neice wore a long veil at her wedding.   <u>niece</u>
3. My nieghbor is trying to lose weight.   <u>neighbor</u>
4. Everyone gives me greif about my height.   <u>grief</u>
5. His neighbor's house is beyond belief.   <u>belief</u>
6. The vain of gold yielded a pound of nuggets.   <u>vein</u>
7. Trying to acheive too much can lead to grief.   <u>achieve</u>
8. She decieved us about how much weight she lost.   <u>deceived</u>
9. His niece is tall enough to reach the cieling.   <u>ceiling</u>
10. A vale of water fell from a great height.   <u>veil</u>
11. "That sign said, 'Yeeld,'" the officer pointed out.   <u>yield</u>
12. The worker siezed the box, despite its weight.   <u>seized</u>

9

Page 10

Review

Directions: Follow the instructions below to see how much you remember from the previous lessons. Can you finish this page correctly without looking back at the other lessons?

1. Write three words that spell /ā/ with ei. <u>vein, veil, reindeer, neighbor, weight</u>

2. Write a word that spells /ī/ with ei. <u>height</u>

3. Write two words that spell /ē/ with ei. <u>deceive, seize, ceiling</u>

4. Write a statement with one subject, two verbs, and an adverb. Mark them S, V, and ADV.

   <u>statements vary</u>

5. Write a question with two subjects, one verb, and an adjective. Mark them S, V, and ADJ.

   <u>questions vary</u>

6. Use the homophone for sealing in a command.

   <u>homophone is ceiling, varies</u>

7. Use the word pronounced /nēs/ in an exclamation:

   <u>niece, varies</u>

8. Finish these sentences in ways that make sense:

The ceiling fell down, but <u>sentences will vary</u>

The ceiling fell down because _____

The ceiling fell down so _____

9. Find three misspelled words and write them correctly.

Todd breefly decieved me about what he was trying to acheive.

<u>briefly deceived achieve</u>

10

74

Spelling Words With /ûr/ And /ôr/

The difference between /ûr/ and /ôr/ is clear in the difference between fur and for.

The /ûr/ sound can be spelled **ur** as in fur, **our** as in journal, **er** as in her, and **ear** as in search.

The /ôr/ sound can be spelled **or** as in for, **our** as in soar, **oar** as in soar, and **ore** as in more.

Directions: Use words from the word box in these exercises.

florist	courtesy	research	emergency	flourish
plural	observe	furnish	tornado	source
ignore	survey	normal	coarse	restore

1. Write each word in the row that names a sound in it. _courtesy, research, flourish,_

/ûr/ _emergency, plural, observe, furnish, survey_

/ôr/ _florist, tornado, source, ignore, normal, coarse, restore_

2. Finish each sentence with a word that has the sound given. Use each word from the word box only once.

We all get along better when we remember to use /ûr/ _courtesy_ .

My brother likes flowers and wants to be a /ôr/ _florist_ .

What was the /ôr/ _source_ of

the /ûr/ _research_ for your report?

For a plural subject, use a /ûr/ _plural_ verb.

He waved at her, but she continued to /ôr/ _ignore_ him.

Beneath the dark clouds was a /ôr/ _tornado_ !

Firefighters are used to handling an /ûr/ _emergency_ .

When will they be able to /ôr/ _restore_ our electricity?

How are you going to /ûr/ _furnish_ your apartment?

11

Creating Word Pictures

Directions: Rewrite each general sentence below two times, giving two different versions of what the sentence could mean. Be sure to use more specific nouns and verbs and add adjectives and adverbs. Similes and metaphors will also help create a picture with words. Notice how much more interesting and informative the two rewritten sentences are in this example:

The animal ate its food.
Like a hungry lion, the starving cocker spaniel wolfed down the entire bowl of food in seconds.
The raccoon delicately washed the berries in the stream before nibbling them slowly, one by one.

1. The person built something.   _sentences will vary_

2. The weather was bad.

3. The boy went down the street.

4. The helpers helped.

5. The bird flew to the tree.

14

Using Similes And Metaphors

A **simile** compares two unlike things using the words **like** or **as**.
For example: The fog was like a blanket around us.

A **metaphor** compares two unlike things without the words **like** or **as**.
For example: The fog was a blanket around us.

"The fog was thick" is not a simile or a metaphor. "Thick" is just an adjective. Similes and metaphors compare two unlike things.

Directions: In each sentence, underline the two unlike things being compared. Then mark the sentence **S** for simile or **M** for metaphor.

_M_ 1. The florist's shop was a summer garden.

_S_ 2. The wood was coarse as sandpaper.

_M_ 3. The survey was a fountain of information.

_S_ 4. Her courtesy was as welcome as a cool breeze on a hot day.

_S_ 5. The room was like a furnace.

Directions: Finish these sentences with similes.

1. The tornado was as dark as _similes will vary_

2. His voice was like _____

3. The emergency was as unexpected as _____

4. The kittens were _____

Directions: Finish these sentences with metaphors.

1. To me, research was _metaphors will vary_

2. The flourishing plants were _____

3. My observation of the hospital was _____

4. Her ignoring me was _____

12

Using Different Forms Of Verbs

To explain what is happening right now, we can use a "plain" verb or we can use **is** or **are** and add **-ing** to a verb.
Like this: We enjoy. They are enjoying.

To explain something that already happened, we can add **-ed** to many verbs or we can use **was** or **were** and add **-ing** to a verb.
Like this: He surveyed. The workers were surveying.

Remember to drop the final **e** on verbs before adding another ending and to add **-es** instead of just **-s** to verbs that end with **sh** or **ch**.
Like this: She is restoring. He furnishes.

Directions: Finish each sentence with the correct form of the verb given. Some sentences already have **is, are, was,** or **were**.

1. The florist is (have) a sale this week. _having_

2. Last night's tornado (destroy) a barn. _destroyed_

3. We are (research) the history of our town. _researching_

4. My mistake was (use) a plural verb instead of a singular one. _using_

5. She (act) quickly in yesterday's emergency. _acted_

6. Our group is (survey) the parents in our community. _surveying_

7. For our last experiment, we (observe) a plant's growth for two weeks. _observed_

8. A local company already (furnish) all of the materials for this project. _furnished_

9. Which dairy (furnish) milk to our cafeteria every day? _furnishes_

10. Just (ignore) the mess in here. _ignore_

11. I get so angry when he (ignore) me. _ignores_

12. Our town is (restore) some old buildings. _restoring_

13. This fern grows and (flourish) in our bathroom. _flourishes_

14. Well, it was (flourish) until I overwatered it. _flourishing_

15

Searching For Synonyms

Directions: In each sentence find a word or group our words that is a synonym for a word in the word box. Circle the word(s) and write the synonym on the line.

florist	courtesy	research	emergency	flourish
plural	observe	furnish	tornado	source
ignore	survey	normal	coarse	restore

1. The children seemed to thrive in their new school. _flourish_

2. Her politeness made me feel welcome. _courtesy_

3. The flower shop was closed when we arrived. _florist_

4. The principal came to watch our class. _observe_

5. Are they going to fix up that old house? _restore_

6. Six weeks after the tornado, the neighborhood looked the same as always again. _normal_

7. What was the origin of that rumor? _source_

8. The whirling storm destroyed two houses. _tornado_

9. She pretended she didn't see me. _ignored_

10. The material had a rough feeling to it. _coarse_

11. Did you fill out your questionnaire yet? _survey_

Directions: Pick three of the words below and write a sentence for each one, showing you know what the word means. Then trade sentences with someone. Do you think your partner understands the words he or she used in sentences?

plural	flourish	source	restore	observe	furnish

1. _sentences will vary_

2. _____

3. _____

13

Describing People

Directions: Often we can show our readers how someone feels by describing how that person looks or what he or she is doing. Read the phrases below. Write in a word or two to show how you think that person feels.

1. Like a tornado, yelling, raised fists: _angry_

2. Slumped, walking slowly, head down: _sad, depressed_

3. Trembling, breathing quickly, like a cornered animal: _scared_

Directions: Write two or three sentences to describe how each person below feels. Don't name any emotions, such as angry, excited, or frightened. Instead, tell how the person looks and what he or she is doing. Create a picture with specific nouns and verbs, plus adjectives, adverbs, similes, and metaphors.

1. a runner who has just won a race for his or her school _sentences will vary_

2. someone on the first day in a new school

3. someone walking down the street and spotting a house on fire

4. a scientist who has just discovered a cure for lung cancer

5. a person being ignored by his or her best friend

16

Spelling Plurals

Is it heros or heroes? Many people aren't sure. Although these rules have exceptions, they will help you spell the plural forms of words that end with o:
- If a word ends with a consonant and o, add -es: heroes.
- If a word ends with a vowel and o, just add -s: radios.

Don't forget other rules for plurals:
- If a word ends with s, ss, z, x, ch, or sh, add -es: buses, classes, quizzes, taxes, peaches, wishes.
- If a word ends with f or fe, drop the f or fe and add -ves: leaf, leaves; wife, wives.
- Some plurals don't end with -s or -es: geese, deer, children.
- The -es rule also applies when a word ending with s, ss, z, x, ch, or sh is used as a verb: kisses, mixes, teaches, pushes.

Directions: Write in the plural forms of the words given.

1. Our area doesn't often have (tornado). _tornadoes_
2. How many (radio) does this store sell every month? _radios_
3. (Radish) are the same color as apples. _Radishes_
4. Does this submarine carry (torpedo)? _torpedoes_
5. Hawaii has a number of active (volcano). _volcanoes_
6. Did you pack (knife) in the picnic basket? _knives_
7. We heard (echo) when we shouted in the canyon. _echoes_
8. Where is the list of (address)? _addresses_

Directions: Write the correct verb forms in these sentences.

1. What will you do when that plant (reach) the ceiling? _reaches_
2. Sometimes my dad (fix) us milkshakes. _fixes_
3. Every night my sister (wish) on the first star she sees. _wishes_
4. Who (furnish) the school with pencils and paper? _furnishes_
5. The author (research) every detail in her books. _researches_

Copyright © 1991 American Education Publishing Co.

17

Review

Directions: Follow the instructions to see how much you remember from the previous lessons. Can you finish this page correctly without looking back at the other lessons?

1. Write three words that have the /ûr/ sound.
   answers will vary
2. Now write three words that have the /ôr/ sound.
   answers will vary
3. Finish this sentence with a simile.
   My bedroom is as neat as _Similies will vary_
4. Finish this sentence with a metaphor.
   My first day at school this year was _metaphors will vary_
5. Use a synonym for crisis in a sentence.
   One synonym is "emergency". Sentences will vary
6. Create a "word picture" based on this sentence:
   The little boy washed his hands.
   "Word pictures" will vary
7. Write two or three sentences describing what a person who is worried about taking a test might look like and do. Show how the person feels without using the word "worried."
   Descriptions will vary
8. Rewrite this sentence, using an -ing form for the verb and the plural form of tornado:
   The winds from the tornado destroyed the trailer park.
   The winds from the tornadoes were destroying the trailer park

Copyright © 1991 American Education Publishing Co.

18

Spelling Words With /kw/, /ks/, And /gz/

The consonant q is always followed by u in words and pronounced /kw/. The letter x can be pronounced /ks/ as in mix, but when x is followed by a vowel, it is usually pronounced /gz/ as in example.

Directions: Use words from the word box in these exercises.

expense	exist	aquarium	acquire	request
exact	expand	exit	quality	excellent
quiz	quantity	exhibit	expression	squirm

1. Write each word in the row that names one of its sounds. (Hint: the h in exhibit is silent.)

/kw/ _aquarium, acquire, request, quality, quiz, quantity, squirm_

/ks/ _expense, expand, excellent, expression_

/gz/ _exist, exact, exit, exhibit_

2. Finish each sentence with a word that has the sound given. Use each word from the word box only once.

We went to the zoo to see the fish /gz/ _exhibit_

I didn't know its /gz/ _exact_ location, so we followed the map.

The zoo plans to /kw/ _acquire_ some sharks for

its /kw/ _aquarium_.

Taking care of sharks is a big /ks/ _expense_, but a number of people

have asked the zoo to /ks/ _expand_ its display of fish.

These people want a better /kw/ _quality_ of fish,

not a bigger /kw/ _quantity_ of them.

I think the zoo already has an /ks/ _excellent_ display.

Some of its rare fish no longer /gz/ _exist_ in the ocean.

Copyright © 1991 American Education Publishing Co.

19

Writing Free Verse

Poems that don't rhyme and don't have a regular rhythm are called "free verse." They often use adjectives, adverbs, similes, and metaphors to create word pictures like this one:

My Old Cat

Curled on my bed at night,
Quietly happy to see me,
Soft, sleepy, relaxed,
A calm island in my life.

Directions: Write your own free verse poems on the topics given.

1. Write a two-line free verse poem about a feeling. Compare it to some kind of food. For example, anger could be a tangle of spaghetti. Give your poem a title.
   poems will vary

2. Think of how someone you know is like a color, sunny like yellow, for example. Write a two-line free verse poem on this topic without naming the person. Don't forget a title.

3. Write a four-line free verse poem, like "My Old Cat" above, that creates a word picture of a day at school.

4. Now write a four-line free verse poem about dreaming at night.

5. Write one more four-line free verse poem, this time about your family.

Copyright © 1991 American Education Publishing Co.

20

Analyzing Words And Their Parts

Remember that a syllable is a word or part of a word with only one vowel sound.

Directions: Use the words from the word box in these exercises.

expense	exist	aquarium	acquire	request
exact	expand	exit	quality	excellent
quiz	quantity	exhibit	expression	squirm

1. Fill in any missing syllables in these words. Then write the number of syllables in each word.

ex _cel_ lent (3)   ac _quire_ (2)   _re_ quest (2)   _squirm_ (1)

qual _ty_ (3)   ex _hib_ it (3)   _ex_ act (2)   _ex_ it (2)

_ex_ pense (2)   _quiz_ (1)   ex _pres_ sion (3)   _ex_ pand (2)

_a_ quar _i_ um (4)   _ex_ ist (2)   quan _ti_ ty (3)

2. Write the word that rhymes with each of these words and phrases.

fizz _quiz_   worm _squirm_   the sand _expand_

resist _exist_   my best _request_   the fence _expense_

in fact _exact_   good fit _exit_   on fire _acquire_

made for me _quality or quantity_   reflection _expression_

it's been sent _excellent_   this is it _exhibit_

3. Write in the word that belongs to the same word family as the one underlined.

I know _exactly_ what I want; I want those ____ shoes. _exact_

Those shoes look _expensive_. Can we afford that ____? _expense_

She wanted us to _express_ ourselves, but she still didn't like my ____. _expression_

When we went to the _exhibition_, I liked the train ____ best. _exhibit_

The museum has a new _acquisition_. I wonder what they ____. _acquired_

Copyright © 1991 American Education Publishing Co.

21

Writing Limericks

Limericks are five-line poems that tend to be silly. Certain lines rhyme, and each line usually has either five or eight syllables, like this:

There once was a young man named Fred	(8 syllables)
Who big muscles went to his head.	(5 syllables)
"I'll make the girls sigh	(5 syllables)
'Cause I'm quite a guy!"	(5 syllables)
But instead the girls all liked Ted!	(8 syllables)

As you can see, all three 8-syllable lines rhyme, and the two 5-syllable lines rhyme.

Directions: Complete the limericks below.

1. There was a young lady from Kent
   Whose drawings were just excellent.
   poem completions will vary

   And to the big city she went.

2. I have a pet squirrel named Squirm

   He ran up a tree
   As far as could be

3. There once was a boy who yelled, "Fire!"

   He just did not see

4. One day I saw my reflection

Copyright © 1991 American Education Publishing Co.

22

76